SOUNDLESS ROAR

Stories, Poems, and Drawings

Ava Kadishson Schieber

with a preface by PHYLLIS LASSNER

NORTHWESTERN UNIVERSITY PRESS
EVANSTON, ILLINOIS

Northwestern University Press
www.nupress.northwestern.edu

Printed in the United States of America

10 9 8 7 6 5 4 3 2 1

ISBN 978-0-8101-3334-1

The Library of Congress has cataloged the original, hardcover edition as
follows:

Schieber, Ava Kadishson.
    Soundless roar : stories, poems, and drawings /
Ava Kadishson Schieber ; with a preface by Phyllis Lassner.
        p. cm.
    Contents: Diary — Love — Children's story —
Rabbit — The party — Trapped — Spirits — Mathilda's
story — Ride into the city — Tzigane — Sultana —
The friend — Dialogue — Farewell.
    ISBN 0-8101-1914-5 (alk. paper)
    1. Schieber, Ava Kadishson. 2. Poets, American—
20th century—Biography. 3. World War, 1939–1945—
Yugoslavia—Poetry. 4. Holocaust, Jewish (1939–1945)—
Yugoslavia. 5. Jewish women—United States—Biography.
6. Holocaust, Jewish (1939–1945)—Poetry. 7. Artists—
United States—Biography. 8. Jews—Yugoslavia—Poetry.
9. Jewish women—Poetry. I. Title.
PS3619.C357Z476 2002
811'.6—dc21 [B]

                                                    2002002402

Frontispiece: Self-portrait of the author at fifteen

dedicated to all who did and still do
teach me to love them

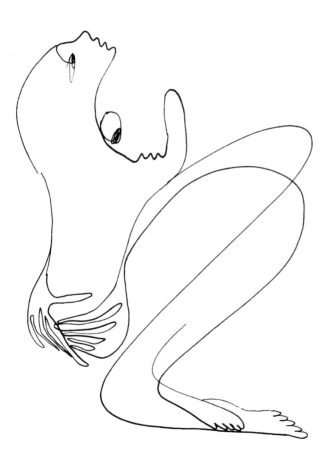

soundless roar the title says
construct your own meaning from the image
of mute din
where a vague maze of lines
limited by size and form
just indicates the space it evolved from
no place to fit a key
mind must break open closed entry
and cross the threshold
stare into obscurity of revealed insight
face glare of unfeigned depths
and then the way back to innocence
has lost all road signs
hence time is nameless too
and word's abundant treasure inadequate
even with novel terms

Contents

Preface

THIS VOLUME INTRODUCES AVA KADISHSON SCHIEBER, a distinctive voice among the tragically few victims who have managed to record their Holocaust experiences. The drawings, stories, and poems in this collection are not, however, her first artistic effort to express her responses to the Nazi death machinery. They represent instead the culmination of many years of artistry—painting and drawing those inconceivable events and losses. Ava's creative drive emerged even during the war, when as a teenager hiding on a small farm in Serbia, with only occasional scraps of paper, she found an outlet to her isolation in drawing. Many years after the war, once she was settled in Israel, she made a career as a set designer at Tel Aviv's Cameri ("Chamber") Theater. But she experienced the need to create a more personal art that would, as she has said, "express the rage" that could have no other voice. And so while her three children were growing up, she began to paint and draw expressionistic renderings that gave a monumental humanity to those the Nazis thought they had dehumanized. In its often strident color and bold lines and brushwork, this art also expressed the emotional process through which she began to cast her wartime memories. Expressing tenderness as well as pain, Ava's painting also memorializes her lost loved ones as the "friendly ghosts" who would always be part of her. In their intertwined figures, the drawings that accompany the following poems and stories show us how these ghosts have become part of who Ava Kadishson Schieber is today.

Ava Hegedish was born in 1926 in Novi Sad, a city about fifty miles north of Belgrade. Her family history reflects the political and cultural turbulence of Central Europe at the time of World War I and its aftermath. Before World War I, Novi Sad had been part of the Austro-Hungarian Empire. Born Leo Herschel, her father changed his name in order to receive a commission in the Austro-Hungarian army and have a better chance of surviving the First

World War. The disguise, however, was also an expression of his identity, for the new name, Hegedish, meaning "violinist" in Hungarian, was also the actual name of a great actor in Budapest. A gifted amateur violinist, Leo Hegedish was also a successful businessman. He saw his playing put to ghoulish use, as Ava was to learn much later and depict in her story "Tzigane": he was forced to play for the Nazis at Auschwitz. Her mother Beatrice, who had been born a Catholic in Vienna, converted to Judaism because of what she felt was its rare integrity in religious and community values. The Jewish community of Novi Sad where Leo and Beatrice began their married life was not large, but prosperous and confident enough that their children could be comfortable making non-Jewish friends. The synagogue they attended, which served the entire Jewish community, was also a cultural and recreation center and contributed to the rich texture of their prewar lives. Ava and her sister, who was five years older, attended the Jewish grammar school, whose high academic reputation spread beyond the Jewish community, attracting the attention of Catholic and Greek Orthodox dignitaries, who decided to send their own children there.

In late 1939, as the family learned from newspapers and the radio about the Nazi takeover of Austria and the invasion of Poland, they deduced that Yugoslavia was not going to escape either. And so they decided to move to Belgrade, where, with its 1 million people, they assumed they had a better chance of blending in and escaping Nazi detection and seizure. For even greater insurance against being identified as Jews, they did not join a synagogue. From her own view of history as deeply connected events, Ava analyzes her parents' decision in light of their experiences of the First World War, which attuned them to signs of political danger. A memory that remains with her from the mid-1930s gives even greater prescience to her parents' intuition. She recalls ships filled with Jews, which instead of coming into harbor were forced to anchor in the middle of the kilometer-wide Danube. As Ava recounts in her video testimony recorded for the Shoah Visual History Foundation, the image of these ships became associated for her with the kind of ghostlike incorporation of lost people that shapes her art. The knowledge of people she couldn't see became embodied in the mythic figure of the flying Dutchman who is doomed to observe ongoing destructiveness, to be a reminder to those who can so easily ignore his warning presence because he cannot make himself felt. Ava's paintings, stories, and poems are a chronicle of looking back and reclaiming those who could not otherwise make themselves felt.

When the Nazis invaded Yugoslavia on April 6, 1941, and the Serbs launched a counterattack, Belgrade was punished with carpet bombing that destroyed the city. Because communication lines were cut, no one was able to know that the Nazis had sliced through Slovenia, and so it was without warning that Belgrade was occupied on April 12. As the homeless masses chaotically sought refuge by taking to the roads leading out of the city, Belgrade's Jews were being systematically rounded up, forced to register their identities, and transported to their doom. Fully recognizing the perfidy behind the Nazi reassurances and promises to send the Jews to labor camps, Leo Hegedish told his wife and daughters that their only chance for survival was to avoid registration, to separate, and to hide. Fearing that he looked too prosperous and too Jewish, that his Serbian was too weak and awkward, Leo escaped to Hungary, where he hoped he could rely on friends and could also help his mother. The fate of Ava's mother Beatrice depended on her original non-Jewish birth certificate which she had kept only as a memento. Ava's sister Susanna escaped attention because of her engagement to a Greek Orthodox man and because a priest falsified her marriage certificate by predating it to the prewar period. Beatrice and her older daughter, whose marriage was then arranged very quickly, hid in various apartments in Belgrade throughout the war. With no access to false papers, Ava was sent by her sister's fiancé to a small farm owned by his Serbian relatives.

Ava speaks of her experiences in hiding as having been in the "anteroom of hell but not hell itself," which she locates in the camps. Isolated on the farm for four years, from the age of fifteen, without parental guidance or the comradeship of her sister or other young people, she paid for her protection by doing manual labor and keeping a low, silent profile. The farmers who harbored her made it all too clear that not only would her cultured speech betray her, but even her city-bred body language. To look people in the eye was a dangerous sign of privilege. "If you have to hide," Ava tells us, "you have to be alone." If you suffered, you could not express your pain for fear of being recognized. And so words could not count as self-expression. At a time when school and friends form the backbone of adolescent development, the young girl who had become "proud and self-sufficient," who had been raised to be independent, chose the only curriculum and companionship available to her. Parcel by parcel, on the road to the farm, she carried her family's *Meyers Lexikon,* the German-language encyclopedia, with which, despite the pigs, chickens, and dogs who shared her living quarters, she built a world of her own.

The experience of being a child of privilege who suddenly found herself a nonperson developed into a sense of time that shapes Ava's stories. As Ava recounts in her video testimony, "The less one is tied to a timetable, the better to adjust to that nonexistence, and to hunger and cold—to feeling useless. Time stopped being meaningful—it became irrelevant. There was no time to be depressed or to indulge in rational thinking." Constant concern about people being killed produced a numbness toward one's surroundings—"a form of psychic death revived only by self-preserving senses. Survival itself became a sharply defined sense." The timetable of Ava's stories often consists of circles within circles, of patterns of an intertwined past, the past present of hiding, and the present looking back at those distinctly separate but inseparable pasts. With full consciousness of her role in authorizing her own memories, she will often begin her stories with an incident from her early childhood that prefigures and shapes the process in which an emotional response to a moment in hiding becomes coherent. Sometimes the narrator's present confronts an image that not only conjures up a moment in hiding but dramatizes its haunting, unanswerable questions. What readers are left with is the sense that these questions constitute the legacy of the Holocaust; circular time is the only way to represent the way the losses of the Holocaust can have no satisfying explanation and no closure. Ava has said that Alfred Adler and Carl Jung have influenced her search for meaning in the question: "How was it possible?" In her visual imagination she sees the process of confronting this impossible question as "corridors to walk through—like Kafka's Castle—where one works oneself through a maze that must end in a cul-de-sac."

We see this inconclusive closure in Ava's stories about the aftermath of the war, when she left the farm and went into Belgrade to find her mother and sister. With snipers and street-to-street fighting still plaguing the city, she made her way to partisan headquarters, where she found no information about her sister, only the certificate of her death. From a friend who had been with her father at Auschwitz she discovered only that he was killed there. Ava and her mother were the family's only survivors. At nineteen, with the responsibility of supporting herself and her mother, who was too weak to work herself, Ava enrolled in the Art Academy of Belgrade and mastered the craft of designing and building miniature models for theatrical sets. Having also learned the art of vigilance, she sensed very quickly the anti-Semitism that had not been vanquished along with the Nazis. As Ava's stories take us into the immediate postwar period, we discover, as she does in a brief encounter with a Jewish Soviet doctor, that it is still expedient to hide one's Jewish identity. The past of Jewish persecution continues its relentless circling once again. No longer the fuel of a death machine, anti-Semitism had evolved into a new form among the allies from the East. As the Soviet armies defeated the Germans and local communist regimes emerged as victors, the new state joined forces with ancient antipathies to reestablish Jewish oppression.

Just as soon as she could muster her artistic and management skills, seizing an opportunity to barter her material inheritance for freedom in 1949, Ava took her mother to Israel. Hitchhiking from their immigrants' tent city in Haifa to Tel Aviv, she presented herself at the Cameri Theater, where they offered to hire her if she could build a model set for their current production. She returned three days later with the completed project and from there continued to design sets, costumes, and theater posters. After only a couple of years, she and her husband opened a theater club that became famous for its introduction of semi-improvisational political satire. By the mid-1950s Ava was exhibiting and selling the paintings that expressed her responses to the events so few were ready to hear about. As hard-hitting as Ava's paintings are, it is remarkable if not paradoxical that they found acceptance at a time when, as so many of them have testified, survivors were being silenced by the caring and well-intentioned, who were encouraging them to put the past behind and build new lives. Ava remembers how people "drifted off, so I stopped talking."

Fifty years later, Ava's stories and poems will find ready listeners. Since moving to the U.S. in the late 1970s, she has already forged powerful connections with audiences through public presentations in schools and community groups. Joining the collective witness and imagined reconstructions of such powerful writers as Ida Fink and Nechama Tec, this volume makes us think not only about the experiences of the Holocaust's hidden children, but how the Holocaust, more than being etched indelibly in memory, forms the post-Holocaust character of its survivors. This dual consciousness has been explored by Charlotte Delbo, whose memoir of Auschwitz distinguished between two memory processes: the memory of the remembering and narrating present and the object of that memory, the "deep memory" of the Holocaust experience which still dominates. The drawings, poems, and stories of Ava Kadishson Schieber find their power in the probing of one memory into another. Just as the artist creates a living past so we have the deep pleasure of reading her. Her art ensures that the memory of Ava's experience will survive in our reading.

—Phyllis Lassner

Acknowledgments

ON MY LENGTHY JOURNEY, rare encounters have enhanced my perspectives. Words of gratitude are but a small homage to the people who have opened a door for me. A long time ago that saved my life. I still consider myself fortunate to meet with inclusion and acceptance and have only words to express my appreciation.

Jacob Lassner extended his scholarly abundance and humanness with a generous welcome to me, including me in his close family enclave.

I am very grateful to Peter Hayes, who gave me through his elegant mind a subtle, indirect encouragement.

How fortunate for me to have Susan Harris as director and editor in chief at Northwestern University Press. I feel privileged to have met her and been invited into her openness to share grief that is but a part of her profuse human realm.

"No one locked in can be released or liberated without help." The reality of ancient experience in this saying out of the Talmud is on my mind when I think about the encouragement I first got from Phyllis Lassner.

My thoughts and verbalized emotions were still in isolated hiding when Phyllis showed interest and offered her deep understanding and knowledge of what I didn't even have a definition for. It was a challenging choice to venture into an unfamiliar medium and express myself in a language recently acquired.

Eager to read more of what I had to say, Phyllis most profoundly encouraged me to continue writing. What a marvelous way to impel anyone's creativity. It became a pleasurable challenge for me to rewrite my stories a couple of times until my language became simpler. Phyllis helped me do this in her unassuming, gentle manner, not impeding my writing—the utmost successful way to teach.

My unabashed gratitude and friendship for Phyllis Lassner.

SOUNDLESS ROAR

moist soft pliable clay
appealed to fingers that formed a bowl
in primal need to play
a tool was made
my own basic hunger sated
I pursue that state
let my hands shape ideas
and mind flare in glare of forms
that float within the real
to find illusion in images I dream of
soothing gentle tender summer rain
as it is drenching downpour I am mostly in
which penetrates below the skin
and leaves me soaked and chilled
my expressions filled with shivers
as much as I try to clad naked forms
the ability to create a canopy of joy
has eluded me
in spite of love for laughter
I am after

DIARY

WHAT STOPPED ME FROM WRITING A DIARY once I knew how to write was that someone could find out how I felt and that would have been embarrassing in the Europe of that time. I was taught shame at an early age. Then, growing up, I learned to enjoy my secrets. If I revealed my innermost thoughts, I would lose some of the power I had gained in my thinking and in controlling my desires and decisions. Of course, those were years of childhood struggles toward adolescence. Later, during the war years in hiding, any written proof that I existed could have been deadly for me and the people who gave me shelter. In hiding, nameless, I was a nonentity.

When the Nazi invasion ended, a new political power took over. It soon became clear to me that there was not too much difference between the totalitarian political rulers and the rules governing totalitarian politics. My war experience had taught me the law of survival. Making myself visible or saying what I believed in would have exposed me to the ever present predators.

My protective shield was silence. I know now how much of our spontaneous reaction to events is lost if not recorded immediately. When I think about my childhood now, I have to trust my memory. How much of reality has remained? What did my brain edit or discard? What is altered to suit my emotional needs at the present time? Regardless, I have to take those chances.

Some years ago, in the northern forest creeks, I witnessed the intensive upstream striving of salmon. For me, that experience meant more than just observing wondrous nature. I, as well as the aquatic life-forms, have the basic dynamic energy to reach for the first memories of life. I, as well as the salmon, have swum the vast oceans of life and overcome a multitude of perils. The salmon migrate to the place where they hatched, urgently rushing there to spawn and die, to close their life cycle—that sight triggered emotions and thoughts about my own symbols of being and dying.

I too have the need to remember people, places, events, and, maybe the most difficult task of all, to recollect past emotions—all this in order to create the close of my own life cycle.

If my childhood was filled with disappointments, I did not believe they were important. I wasn't sad for long. My earliest recollection of perpetual joy was sitting under the square table in the dining room. It was not merely a large table covered with a silky velour cloth, with its rich autumn colors and fringes that reached the carpet. This was my private world that nobody could invade. As I crawled through the fringes, sights and sounds diminished—I entered my enclave. The table had heavy legs carved of dark wood. They were reinforced on the lower part by planks that met in the center and were topped with a smooth wooden ball. I loved to sit on the planks, hugging that wooden center piece with both hands. It was the steering wheel into a world where it was up to me to decide where to turn; or to drift where my fancy would take me. My feet comfortably on the floor, I enjoyed the journeys. I remember the smell of turpentine and the linseed oil varnish with which the table was regularly polished. Might this have been the smell that made me decide to became a painter at the end of the war, that time when I had to decide upon my studies?

In early childhood, my fantasies must have been part of the fairy tales Mother read regularly to my sister Susanna and me. A frequent daydream of mine was about the river Danube, especially in the way it regularly flooded the countryside. In my fancy, the water would reach the grounds we lived on, and I would swim in our dining room. Later my imagination became more extravagant. I would be on an expedition, riding on an elephant in a dense jungle, with lots of adventures, just as I had seen in the movies. There were also fears in my jungle game. At that time, though, horror was fascinating, because it was only a game; I could go in any direction of my terror-filled fantasies and return safely into my secure surroundings. I believed that angry-looking people could, magically, turn into animals with shrill voices and attack me. I sensed evil abounding in the real world. As a small child, I had a simple image about the look and sound of menacing people. Years later, I learned what really dangerous faces looked like. People in splendid attire, elegant, with shining boots and spotless kid gloves, people who spoke with gentle, educated voices, who listened to beautiful music and could even smile—these were the villains who were out to kill me.

I don't think that childhood fantasy of protecting myself, of hiding under the table, was a premonition of the years ahead. No horror-ridden conjecture could have suggested the reality that was to follow. There was childhood, and then instant maturity.

My childhood routine, finding comfort under the dining room table, must have started after Grandfather died. He was the person who always had time for me. He used to sit in his armchair all day long; maybe there was no place else for him to go after he had lost all his assets. That, of course, was a story I must have heard later on. My earliest memories are connected with Grandfather Leib. He knew how to make me laugh, telling stories with funny words I did not understand; he used to laugh when everyone else seemed annoyed most of the time. The more serious Grandmother would become, the more comical the whole story appeared. He always smiled when he talked to me, and his face would go askew—his mustache would turn up on one side while the other half would droop. I always had to laugh when his face twisted around in that way. He also used to sing to me. The words of his songs must have had nasty meanings, because Grandmother would voice her indignation and Mother's face would get red, and we would laugh.

Grandfather gave me a special name, and that was really important. He was the only who used it—Shahorith Pincales. It sounded grandiose and I was proud. He used to sing songs with my name and make me learn the words. Encouraging me even more, Grandfather taught me to make accompanying sounds by using pot lids as percussion; we were noisy in our fun. For another of our entertainments, when someone walked past his armchair he would extend his long legs. My mother, always in a hurry, would stumble regularly over his outstretched feet. She was the frequent victim of his joke, yet she accepted it without showing any annoyance as we laughed. Maybe she needed some amusement as well, even when it was at her own expense.

I remember Grandfather's death. Even today, I have a vivid image of the apartment our family occupied at that time. The small cozy rooms, with sunlight penetrating only in the morning because we were on the ground floor. After Grandfather's death we moved to a larger place.

He died when I was around two or three. I remember the sunshine through the lace curtain, making a partial pattern on the bed where Grandfather was leaning on many pillows. The room was filled with people. Someone must have put me on the bed, and Grandfather smiled at me as he always did. Then Mother lifted me and took me out of the room. She said Grandfather was dying.

I didn't know what that meant until much later, when I realized that dead meant gone, never to return. The memory of that event, just before he died, remained clear whenever I thought about Grandfather. I understood years later, when I was confronted and surrounded by death, that he had left the most valuable legacy he could ever have given me. His smile erased terror from my own thoughts of dying. It helped me to accept life.

In the house where I grew up, the furniture belonged to my grandparents. It was carefully chosen when they got married, with good taste and a lot of money. They both belonged to the emerging world of Eastern European Jewish merchant affluence. Because they were related, the family fortune was not divided when they married.

There was a lot of silver and fine glass in the house, and beautifully embroidered linens. That was all that remained of their pre–World War I world. With the fall of the Austro-Hungarian Empire, the family business was completely destroyed. As loyal citizens, my grandparents had put all their wealth into government bonds, which became a pack of useless paper when the government fell.

Later on, that fact was mentioned more in connection with war in general. If it was the intention to teach us children a lesson in history and finance, it served its purpose well.

It was in their prime that my grandparents lost all their means and dreams. That was at the beginning of the century. Then, three decades later, Grandmother saw herself that she and even her grandchildren were chosen to be victims once again.

A new generation descended from the old Austro-Hungarian Empire came back to the place of former defeat. Only this time, the new conquerors came back not only to loot but to kill us as well. In my early childhood there were people all over who had tried to live in spite of the painful wounds life had inflicted on them. Their injuries and fears were disguised, yet evident. Years later I understood that real terror never heals. It compounds.

The name Grandfather gave me is still with me. It took decades until I could understand the message it expressed, and what the name he gave me meant to him. Shahorith is the morning prayer and Pincale is a tiny bundle.

I was Grandfather's bundle of morning joy.

stay alive and I will find you
when battles are over
even though wars never end
we will pretend an illusion of peace
I was hidden in this
rage-ridden region
until the deadly violent reign
did wane
it was not known
when or where you were killed
I stayed alive
filled with memories and longing
long after trees matured
on forgotten mounds
of burial grounds

LOVE

I T WAS THE FIRST TIME I FELT LOVE for someone who was not my family. His name was Ferko. He had large dark eyes and a gentle smile. Ferko arrived with his mother one summer to visit someone who lived in the large building where we had an apartment. Both Ferko and I were preschoolers. Because I was the youngest, none of the neighbors' children wanted to play with me. Ferko was much taller than I, but he was a stranger, an outsider— no one wanted him either. Though he and his mother came from a neighboring country, he was not the least bit proficient in the Serbian language we spoke. That didn't matter to us. We became inseparable. It was love. We didn't even mind that the bigger children teased us about it. My parents, however, did not laugh when I said that Ferko and I were going to get married when we grew up.

At the end of that summer, Ferko told me that he and his mother were leaving Novi Sad. They had come to visit and hoped to stay, but it hadn't worked out. They had to depart. He was very serious when he said that he believed he would be back next summer. We held hands until he had to go. We were both sad.

Next summer was disappointing for me. I had anticipated seeing Ferko again, but he and his mother never returned.

I started school that fall. None of the boys even slightly resembled Ferko. The boys in my class were boisterous and conceited, the opposite of Ferko, with his gentle manners, and none of them had beautiful dark eyes.

It was some years later that I was in love again. His name was Paul and he had velvety dark eyes and a gentle smile. I noticed that the first time I met him. Paul was four years older than I and that was unusual for a high school romance. It took me a whole school year to make Paul aware of my existence. When he did, we developed a serious, captivating friendship. Neither his friends nor his family could separate us.

In the year before the war invaded our area, I had to join my parents, who had moved to Belgrade. Paul had to stay in Novi Sad to graduate. We were in love, but when the war started we lost each other. And prewar circumstances had already initiated the separation.

During that year I moved beyond my high school romance with Paul. I met Vojislav in Belgrade. My sister was engaged to be married to a Greek Orthodox Serb and one day my future brother-in-law brought his young friend to our house. Vojislav had just graduated from Belgrade University in mathematics. In order to remain in the city he had to work. It was also politically essential for him to stay in the capital because he was already a political outcast. I understood the urgency of Vojislav's not going back to his native village. And so it was easy to convince me to take private math lessons with him.

Voja was good-looking and very serious. From our first meeting, I was intrigued by someone not only so much more mature than I, but a person in hiding, a political exile. We Jews were already outlawed and were being killed in most parts of Europe at that time. So it was no wonder that I felt kinship and fell in love with this man. I was even ready to study extra math. The lessons Voja gave me were really lectures in understanding the political situation that was overtaking Europe; there would be manipulations to which we all were going to succumb. Voja was eager to make me grasp what was going to happen in the approaching conflict. He talked about precautions to help us survive even if we were hunted down. For me at that time, however, the touching of our knees under the table seemed the most important reality.

But Voja's seriousness about the political situation did in a way sink in. I was just beginning to experience how beautiful it was to be young, but that time was obviously dwindling away. Even though we never met except during my lessons, we grew close. Then just before the city was bombed and destroyed, Voja said: "Stay alive and I will find you when the war is over."

I knew, when we parted, he meant what he said. He was standing in the doorway, reluctant to leave, holding my hand, then sheltering it with his other hand in an attempt to protect me. I had not yet realized that we might not see each other for a long time. Voja hugged and kissed me. It was the first time I had kissed, and the sensation rushed through my whole being. I never saw him again, but Voja never completely left my memory.

Four years later, when the fighting was over, after lengthy inquiries at the partisan headquarters I got the answer—Voja was killed in the second year of the war.

In 1945 I started to search for all the people I desperately hoped to find. Inquiries in Belgrade were discouraging. It was about that time that I could finally go to Novi Sad. Everything that had existed in my life just four years earlier seemed distanced by decades.

In Novi Sad I looked for my father and grandmother, my former school friends, and Paul as well. It soon became clear that people who did not return from the concentration camps or who did not come out of hiding must have been killed. Except for my mother, everyone I loved was dead. Novi Sad was a painful memory, and I stayed only a couple of days and headed back to Belgrade.

After being liberated from the horrifying fear for my life, I felt the energy of youth, of being alive and facing the future. I even had some dreams that, in their primordial forms, expelled recurring nightmares. In spite of all the difficulties any survivor had to face at the end of the war, I had hopes for an easier time. First, it was essential to find work to continue my education. I had basic expenses and absolutely no other source of income. Weakened by the wartime experience, my mother was now totally dependent on me and I had to take care of her. Instead of making me feel overwhelmed, though, the responsibility for her well-being helped me to create my own frame of behavior and stay afloat in this novel, unfamiliar, puzzling life after the war. I did not feel appreciated, even accepted, in this postwar society. I was not the outcast I had been during Nazi occupation, but I was an outsider, not to be integrated.

I heard there was a need to help reorganize the Jewish Community Center in Belgrade, the only place where I didn't feel rejected. Immediately after the war, there were very few Jewish survivors and none from my generation. Most of the people at the Belgrade Jewish Community Center were middle-aged and from mixed marriages; they had survived the war in hiding. For all of us, the Jewish Community Center became a haven, a place of nourishment. Mother started to volunteer at their kitchen, so at least we sometimes had free meals.

I was asked to volunteer at the Center's makeshift infirmary because of my experience helping in other improvised infirmaries during the fighting. Most of those temporary hospitals were located in schools, under horribly primitive conditions, with extremely poor chances of healing anyone. I learned how resilient life could be. At times I was the only one to help the overworked but highly dedicated nuns, who with no opiates were bravely ameliorating suffering and closing dead eyes.

At the Jewish Community Center I was already known by some of the attending medical staff for not fainting at the painfully awful sights we were confronted with, as when we took care of people with amputated limbs and gaping wounds. Having earned a reputation for a stoic presence, I was asked by Dr. Alkalay, the former chief rabbi of Belgrade, to help out. The Center had become an improvised station for Jewish refugees. Among them were survivors of Nazi forced labor camps in southern Serbia who were in transit to Central Europe. They were the few coming back from the notorious copper mines of Bor.

I remembered that name—Bor—from my childhood before the war. Bor was an infamous place even in time of peace. Mining in Bor equaled punishment. No one who worked its mines lived very long. Before the occupation only those desperate enough or those who did not know better worked the copper mines. The Nazis used it as one of their working hell camps. We anticipated facing the survivors of Bor with trepidation; most of them, we had heard, were in serious condition, barely able to make the journey to Belgrade. I had seen soldiers with gaping wounds and exposed bones. I had learned to marvel at the stoic acceptance of pain and death. This time it was different.

The people we were waiting for had not been soldiers fighting a war. They were doomed because they were Jews, and some had been teenagers when they were sent into the mines. After the need for their labor ceased, they became useless, disposable for the oppressor, and were left to die. We had just that much information.

I knew I was going to be involved with each one of the survivors of Bor. The persecution of all Jews had greatly fortified my sense of belonging. We prepared army cots in the big hall of the Center. Linen was scarce, but we washed and scrubbed and were excited about receiving the few precious survivors. Some arrived on stretchers; some could barely walk. Only two young men were in good condition. They were the heroes who had made the transport possible—Stephan Kroh and Martin Goldberg.

Stephan and Martin had helped the whole group stay alive after the Nazi guards fled. Not having left themselves enough time to kill the inmates, the German guards had run, leaving the dead and dying. It was fortunate that Stephan and Martin were healthy and strong enough and able to steal food from peasants in the area. None of the others could have gone out on those nightly raids. With peasants shooting at the intruders, they would inevitably have starved to death. Stephan and Martin fed their fellow inmates and held on until they got through to a makeshift medical transport.

At least some in the group were still alive, and they arrived with the Red Cross in Belgrade. On one of the vans was a man whose skin had the pallor of ebbing life. He had the most beautiful face I had ever seen. I was walking beside the stretcher, captivated. He had a very dark beard and hair. When the men lifted his frail body from the stretcher onto the bed, there was a faint moan and the man opened his eyes. They were deep dark pools. I knew why I could not pull myself away. I had known that face all my life. I whispered "Ferko," and though there was only a dim smile on the man's face, it lit up his eyes. He might not have recognized me, but he remembered the name he had not heard for a long time.

I don't know if I cried, as there were no tears in me. I do remember kneeling at the side of his cot, putting my cheek on the pale hand in a desperate hope to transfer some of my vitality to the dying body. He looked at peace, but there seemed so little hope for recovery.

My two helpers introduced themselves as Stephan and Martin. They were astonished that I knew the man by his childhood nickname, Ferko. They had only known him as Ference. At that stage Ferko could not speak anymore, but would just look at me and follow me with his eyes when I moved away. I asked to be excused from other duties as much as possible because I wanted to sit beside Ferko and hold his cool hand, where there was still some life pulsing under the pale skin.

I knew he was dying, and so did he. We were the generation of realists. I was sitting beside Ferko's bed, telling him first about my prewar school years, and then about my life during the war, hiding on a farm. I was aware that he didn't understand what I said, but my voice must have been a soporific, because he fell into a quiet sleep. Dr. Alkalay told me there was no hope for Ferko's recovery and excused me from any other work. I could stay beside my friend as long as I wished. It was good to keep him at peace, because we were without any medications to ease anyone's pain.

During the night vigil I must have occasionally fallen asleep sitting in the chair. Awake, I would listen to Ferko's uneven breathing.

His life was slipping away. The only vital sign the next day was the movement of his nostrils so that he could inhale some oxygen. I was not capable of leaving him. I couldn't let go of his hand while there was still blood slowly pulsing through the person with whom my own life was so closely connected. Two days after they had all arrived, Ferko died very peacefully. He just stopped breathing. I was holding on to his hand until it became completely cold.

That day Dr. Alkalay told me to take Stephan and Martin to my home. I managed to get more food than we were usually able to in order to make dinner for the two young men. After all, they had bravely rescued all those who could not have made the journey without their help. And they were shattered that Ferko could not be saved. I was numb. After my vigil I also needed to connect with life again, so the three of us headed for my home. On the way, I told them about my childhood encounter with Ferko. They all came from the same area, the Carpathian region. My mother made a beautiful meal that night, serving it on the only tablecloth we had left. I understood why Dr. Alkalay had insisted that I bring Stephan and Martin to a home atmosphere. The experience of being part of a family reached far beyond the meagerness of the meal we were able to offer.

Every day after that evening, when I was finished with my work at the infirmary, both Stephan and Martin escorted me home. And of course I invited them up. Experts in organizing food, Stephan and Martin always brought some delicious varieties in the big pockets of their army coats. For a couple of weeks, we had a beautiful friendship.

Then came the time of departure. Several days before they were to leave, Stephan said he was going to come back and marry me. I knew he meant it. Martin was afraid Stephan was going to stay in Belgrade at that point and not join him and the transport for the rest of the journey home. Stephan was reluctant to leave, and begged me to come along with them and the transport of remaining repatriates. He tried to convince me and everyone else that there was a crying need for nursing help.

Dr. Alkalay, whom I asked about this whole project, said: "How will you live with yourself if you leave your mother now?" His words deeply affected the little bit of sanity that was still left in me.

There had been so many losses, I was desperate to reconnect with life—and here was Stephan Kroh, young and healthy, good-looking, in love with me and full of vitality. I wanted to leave all the unmarked graves I had accumulated over the last couple of years. I wanted to hold on to a live hand that made my own blood flow. But there was the voice of reason and reality—I stayed.

After some months a Russian soldier came to look for me. He had my address on a letter he was carrying. The letter was from Stephan. I asked the soldier in to have a bite with Mother and me; he must have been away from home a long time and I could see that he was so happy to be invited. Russian soldiers were not welcomed into homes. The soldier remained silent throughout the meal.

Stephan had written me a beautiful love letter. It was half in the Serbian he had picked up and half in Slovak. The letter was in an envelope smeared with mud, and when I looked carefully I realized that the mud was mixed with blood.

Before the Russian soldier left, he thanked us for our hospitality and tears were running down his cheeks. I asked him if Stephan Kroh was dead. He was.

I still want to witness
how light transforms
hounding shadows cast from giant massifs
as a child I feared the angry mountain
where clouds like shrouds
embraced green forests
with gray menacing grief
forecasting storms
now many roaring thunders later
I welcome the life-giving lashing rain
stripping the air naked
sending sensuous scents of dawn
I wait for the dark blue sky
to pale into yellow
with a ray of day

CHILDREN'S STORY

MOTHER WAS A PROFOUND BELIEVER. She believed in the crisp cold winter air and steamed vegetables, and she believed in books as an enhancing element of life. Later on when I was by myself, I discovered the diversity of ideas put into words. It was then that I started to wonder about her indiscriminate insatiable appetite for the joy of print. Throughout the years, Mother didn't share the wasteful amount of information she gathered with such ardor. It is true, I had never asked her to do so—I had been so involved in my own activity of being. At that time, when I was just beginning to grow up, the world around me already showed harbingers of the change that followed; this was to be a time when one had to depend more on oneself.

There were all kinds of rituals Mother used to practice and in which I was supposed to participate. The ones that I found most likable were those I must have accepted as ordinary, obvious events of life. I remember those I disliked. One was almost a daily winter routine. First—I did not like winter. Whenever the weather permitted, we took lengthy walks through the crunching snow. While Mother regarded this as healthy, I just felt that the cold added frostbite to my usually numb fingers and toes.

And then there was the reading of fairy tale books. I loathed those fairy tales. They became the ritual practice for exceptionally harsh weather, when even Mother was willing to stay indoors. She would bundle up me and my sister—woolen hats and all—put us into her big bed and cover us with the heavy down comforter, the only redeeming feature in the procedure.

Then Mother would open the windows with great determination. I would wait for her steaming breath in the icy air, the precursors of even frostier details creeping out of those fairy tale books. The stories were overloaded with cannibalistic giants who roamed dark wooded mountaintops. As you might expect, their preferred diet consisted of small children. This fantasy must have influenced my distaste for meat.

All the children in those stories were unfortunate, as their mothers died very young. Later on it occurred to me that the storytellers must have had grudges against mothers and women altogether, since the stepmothers of those wretched orphans were always witches. When Mother read those stories for the first time, I heard mostly the horror and misery. Later on I knew better. I heard Mother's voice, but not what she said. That was the beginning of my disregard, my not listening to what I do not want to hear. I have never lost that aptitude. Sometimes I wonder whether I have developed this shortcoming into an asset.

In those early encounters with violence in books, I indulged myself by ignoring the words that induced fear. Later I learned how words could often be forerunners of fearful events. The atrocious reality that took place when I was growing up lay far beyond any of the nightmarish fantasies of those children's horror tales.

During the wartime years, I had to hide in order to stay alive. In those times, I used to imagine I was like a child in a horror fairy tale, running through forests to save my life. Only now, the menacing creatures were real and so was the efficient mass killing. In those dreadful times I often thought about the cannibalistic giants who lived on the dark mountaintops of fairy tales. The descendants of those childhood story monsters did not eat the lot. They just murdered millions. The event labeled by history as World War II has engaged many minds who try to understand or interpret such destructive behavior. Yet no one has been able to supply or invent an explanation—how it was possible for the Holocaust to occur—how bystanders could allow such unthinkable cruelties. We grown-up people do what a small child discovers—it is easier not to listen to what is horrifying. We turn deaf whenever we choose. There is an end to every frightening fairy tale—till the next one starts.

In my childhood, the story I liked to listen to was that of "The Warty Frog." It had the predictable "Once upon a time" beginning, with the usual trimmings—a good and loving mother who dies; an evil witch who enters with her spells and black magic. Those fairy tale kings must have been simpletons, as they all married atrocious ladies. As a child, it was disquieting for me to accept that people of high standing and responsibilities such as went with being a king could show such poor judgment.

In the one story I liked, the towering envious queen stepmother was throwing warty frogs into the poor orphaned princess's bathwater. In spite of my affection for animals, this struck me as an unpleasant mental image. Frogs in a bathtub. The queen wanted to cover the beautiful child with frog's skin. But the princess had magic of her own. She was good and kind, and these qualities endowed her with a different sort of power. She could turn warty frogs into water lilies. I liked that. I still love flowers emerging out of ponds. There were marshes near my childhood home. The water level of the pond nearby was influenced by the movement of the big river that flooded regularly every spring. When I would venture over to the pond, I could recognize the tadpoles and follow their growing stages within the still water. It would have made me very happy to have seen at least one flower, but there were no water lilies in those swampy ponds. A flower would have been a sign of some good magic.

Some years later, when I was becoming a teenager, I was allowed to take a rowboat into the river branches that stretched like fingers from the main stream of the Danube. I remember the stillness and smell of decay in the air, the quiet parting of the opaque greenish water, where large frogs glided silently into the water from the roots of the trees. Those roots were so intertwined that the trees supported each other, combating the element that nourished them and yet destroyed their existence at the same time. There were no flowers. No flowers ever grew out of those murky waters. During the war years many people were killed on the banks of the Danube. Herded in masses—killed and pushed into the river. Flowers and buds as well as bodies were buried under the ice only to emerge between the flooded roots in spring. I never want to go back to the Danube.

In my nightmares I used to sit in my boat and wait for a movement in the water. And then I would see armies of frogs emerging behind the tree roots and out of the mud. They would advance, multiplying in numbers and growing to gigantic sizes. They would glide into the water from all sides until I was surrounded. The monstrous creatures would look at me with expressionless glares. That scene reappeared in my dreams again and again, as did the terror of being caught by the overpowering creatures. I would see outlines of sunken flowers underneath the water's surface.

Flowers that will never emerge or grow. That was reality—not a fairy tale. I know that warty frogs will never develop into water lilies—but I am still the child that waits for such a miracle.

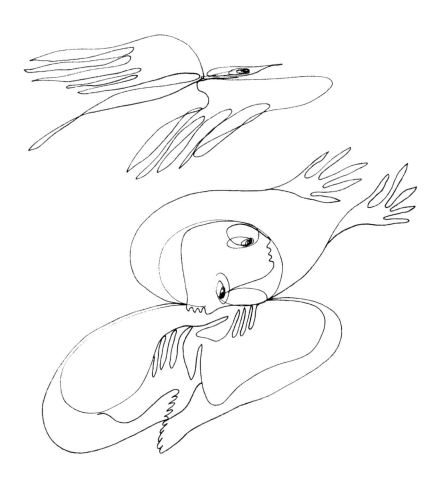

I bury my dead and try to do it fast
while memory is fresh with life's vigor
and trust not an embalmed image
to cast a rigid mockery
a child with no understanding
I hugged my rabbit to death
and learned there was no mending
with life gone

RABBIT

AS A SMALL CHILD I THOUGHT that grandmothers were the heads of families. In our household, my grandmother was the one who used to make all the important decisions. Everyone depended on her for advice and she made things happen. Her specialty was taking care of the family's finances. Grandmother Hermina must have known how to manage money, because this was a time when most people had not only lost their means and savings during World War I, but were lost themselves. Her ability was evident, even decades later, when members of our more distant family would visit and talk, not about their lives in the present, but about the fortunes they had lost because of the first war.

Grandmother never complained about or offered any details of the financial losses she and Grandfather suffered. When the Austro-Hungarian Empire was defeated in 1918, anyone who had invested in government bonds was wiped out. "One had to, and did, create resources," Oma, as my sister and I used to call Grandmother, would say. She would then offer a short explanation, but focusing primarily on the political consequences of the historical events: After Austria-Hungary lost the war in 1918, new countries were carved out of it. Where we lived became Yugoslavia, and with it, reality changed. These were explanations that may not have been the blueprint for a carefree childhood, but were great lessons for a child to learn about the unpredictability of life and politics.

Oma seemed to sail like a flagship through rough times. She knew how to navigate, on an even keel, head high, without being the least bit haughty. If my sister and I would complain, she used to say: "Do not lament, as no one will listen anyway—it is futile and very boring." In spite of her unyielding ways, she knew enough to listen when I had something to say. There is no doubt that this sensitivity brought me close to her. Oma made it clear, as small as I was, that I was an important person, and my opinion was to be considered.

Many years later, after she was gone out of my life and I was grown up, I realized what a great lady my grandmother had been.

Now I am about the age Grandmother was just before the beginning of the Second World War. Back then, two generations apart seemed like such a far distance in time. After all those past decades, ever since she was deported by the Nazis and then killed, I still feel so very emotionally close to her. It was difficult for me to part with her when my parents and sister decided to leave Novi Sad, our hometown. Oma remained in the house where we had all lived together. I never did see her again, because the war started soon after we left.

There are but fragments in my mind about her from that prewar time. Most certainly I have no information about Grandmother's youth, but I remember her as always being so alive and active. My sadness about her now is because I could have at least learned so much from her about her youth when we were together. So I regret not having asked her when I had all those opportunities. If she had been asked, she probably would have been as bluntly honest in telling her story as she was about everything else. I still try to figure out what Grandmother's growing up might have been like. It's like trying to fill in all the blank spaces of an ancient fresco on a wall of an excavation site, where almost all of the image has disintegrated.

I do know this. She was the only girl among four brothers who lived together with their mother. While her children were still small, my great-grandmother had thrown her husband out of the house. Amazingly for that time, she brought up her children alone and all of them finished school; this must have been an enormous task, not to mention a huge achievement. This story, compressed and summarized, was all I ever heard about Grossi, as we called the regal old lady, who later lived in our household. Until her death, just a couple of years before the war started, she used to read the newspapers that were printed in Hebrew letters in Vienna. With such a role model, so informed about political events, I was proud of being a girl.

Now I am back in time, in the thirties, before the Second World War. Ominous signs were already everywhere. Hatred of the Jews in Germany was rampant and spreading. It was amazing how it seemed easy to hate. A whole civilized nation erupted into berserk hysteria, and blind madness celebrated hatred.

One summer, a decade before the actual war started, Grandmother decided to take my sister and me to visit her relatives who owned a farm. This may have been a gesture to compensate for one of those restrictions by which everything in our home had to accommodate Grandmother. The visit may also have been intended to compensate us urban children for our unfulfilled longing for contact with animals, or maybe it was just one of her educational endeavors to show my sister that there was life beyond our comfortable city. Some members of the larger family called the farming relatives the Peasants. Oma resented that. "Only ignorant snobs believe somebody else is inferior because of what they do for a living." She made that lesson dramatically clear to us children.

I was not yet in school and tried very hard to belong to the world I realized was so much larger than anything that I could imagine. Much of my surroundings was rather indifferent toward me. It was frightening to be so unimportant. I remember my awareness of events all around us, changes that worried the grown-ups and that produced the threatening aura I used to feel and fear like the tension that held the air before big storms.

Just as Oma had planned, we had our summer vacation on the farm. My first memory of arriving in the country and on the farm was the horrible odor. I was told that it came from the slaughterhouse and also from the tannery, both of which were adjacent to the farm. The explanation did not make it any more tolerable. But after a couple of days it did not disturb me any more. I had learned that I could even get used to something disgusting.

Around the farm there were large workhorses that I was allowed to ride. I loved the towering position I held while sitting on their backs and have loved horses ever since. Another treat while we were at the farm was receiving a small rabbit as a gift. It was the most precious toy I ever had because this one was alive. I was so proud to be entrusted with its care. Oma told me not to get too attached to my rabbit and she cautioned me to lift my pet only by its ears. This way of handling the rabbit seemed to me a very cruel thing to do; how would I feel being pulled up by my ears? I remember how everyone laughed when I said that—and I remember my embarrassment at being laughed at.

The farm animals were not pets, I was told. They were grown and sold for meat and to produce leather for the tannery. The slaughter was disturbing—even after I had grown used to the smell. I must have started to recognize and perhaps even confront many distressing facts as being part of life. When we were in the city, I used to accompany Grandmother and our maid, Paula, to the market and I liked its loud and tumultuous activity, liked going from stall to stall, bargaining and buying. These trips taught me how to select foods for freshness and variety. I never thought of the live chickens and geese we bought as becoming meat on my plate. Fish had to be chosen while they were swimming in water tanks; then they were hit on the head, and finally wrapped in newspaper to be carried home. When I complained on behalf of the fish— which, unlike the chicken and geese, I only thought of as having been hurt—I was told that the reason they were hit on the head was so they wouldn't jump out of Paula's basket.

At the mealtime gatherings of our hosts and ourselves, the guests, there were lengthy talks about politics. Our relatives were extremely worried, especially the son and daughter, who both wanted to get married. They were concerned because animosity against the Jews was already spreading beyond the border of Germany into the Yugoslav countryside—they felt the undercurrent of hatred that emanated from the neighboring farmers, mostly of German or Hungarian descent. The selling of farm products was becoming difficult. Even selling the land was not possible.

My attention span for world events, and even local politics, must have been marginal. My memory is only of the two young people who were talking about being completely isolated from their former friends. Because they were no longer invited anywhere, they seemed sad to me.

After a couple of days of being carried around all day long—I couldn't part with my lovable toy—my fluffy gray rabbit died. I was devastated when I was told that hugging my rabbit all the time must have compressed its lungs. What the animal needed was to be lifted by its ears and left alone. A live rabbit was not a toy. No one was angry or even reproached me. The rabbit was just another animal on the farm, but nevertheless, I wasn't given another pet. Nothing else mattered for the rest of the summer.

Years later the war reached my home ground. Suddenly it was all swept away, like a sand castle caught up in a stream of horror. I had to leave everything that my life had been; I went into hiding. The people who gave me shelter owned a small farm not far from Belgrade. Because they hated the Nazi invaders, they were ready to risk themselves and hide a Jew. I felt very grateful to these strangers who took me in. But there were no rabbits on the farm and I was no child anymore. The next stage of my life, my teenage years, were the war years, spent in hiding.

At the beginning of the Nazi occupation there was still a week or two before it became extremely hazardous to go back and forth into the city of Belgrade. Due to the terrible destruction in those first days, caused by the German bombers, the city was in utter chaos. Thousands of victims were buried under the rubble. Some might have still been alive, trapped in the ruins, but no one tried to clear the debris and look for survivors. Instead there was looting of whatever was at hand. Large crowds were leaving the devastated city, and I felt reasonably safe so long as I moved with the streams of people.

Taking valuables from our apartment in the city to the farm, like so many refugees, I was loaded with heavy packages. Crystal, silver, fine linen, all acquired over many years for my sister's and my trousseaux. Except for the books I took for myself, my family agreed to let the farmers have everything I brought to the farm. Books would have been useless to them, but for the duration of the war, with no possibility for me to continue my education, those books represented my identity and link to the home that did not exist anymore. In a way I believe they preserved my sanity.

I had said good-bye to everyone and everything I loved, that entire part of my life that gave me security. Hiding meant entering a frightening, lonesome existence. In this time of war, with staying alive being my only concern, and being gravely deprived of food, loneliness was not the primary focus. By the time I became aware of my isolation, it already had been compounded into gargantuan proportions.

It was the end of April 1941 when I parted from my father, never to see him again. On occasion, during the war, I was able to meet my mother and sister, but leaving the relative safety of the farm was always dangerous. There was always the possibility of being stopped by any authority in the city and being asked for identification papers. I knew this risk was the price for seeing Mother and my sister.

As the war continued, my fears of confronting a roadblock subsided; moreover, my life had become so insignificant, I was ready to risk it. The most difficult time of adjustment was at the beginning, when I was forced to accept the enormous change in my whole reality, and the unaccustomed and difficult physical work expected of me. Adding to the burden of my heavy chores was the realization that I was homeless, nameless, isolated from talking to anyone. But despite this confrontation with an unknown and unwelcome reality, I felt gratitude toward the people who gave me shelter. I gave my best with no complaints.

On the farm, water drawn from the well was not safe to drink. It was for washing, for the animals, for doing the laundry—all of these my responsibilities. One of the difficult tasks in my new life was to go up and down the nearby hills, fetching drinking water from the spring. It was a long walk over rolling hills, especially with the weight of the water cans. At times I went more than once a day, hot in summer, my fingers freezing in winter. There were several routes I could take and their diverse scenery compensated for the longer ones I sometimes chose.

One detour I particularly liked brought me close to a house where I noticed two small children; after observing them a few times, it became clear to me that like me, they had not been born on a farm. I concluded that the children were there because they were being hidden from the Nazi occupier. Needless to say, I tried to get a look at them in such a way as not to arouse suspicion. The wisest plan I could think of was to pass by the house while I was loaded down with cans of water. Back at my own farm hideout, I explained why I had changed my route and the extra time it took. It turned out that though she usually didn't talk much, the young woman farmer knew everything that was going on in the village and the surrounding area. In this case, because she understood my curiosity, she was willing to tell me what she had heard about the children I had seen.

The parents of the two children — a girl of just about preschool age and the boy a toddler — had escaped from countries already occupied by the Nazis. They had arrived before the war reached Serbia, and now were hoping to take advantage of the fact that there were some routes that were still open to the south of the Balkan Peninsula. If they could manage it, they intended to board a ship and try to reach Italy. In the meantime, the children had been left on the farm in care of the woman who owned it. "For a big sum," my farmer said.

Accompanying me on my lookout for the two children was my dog Paca, who accompanied me on my daily water-fetching excursions. He was the youngest of the four dogs who shared my room in the small shack beside the pigsty and the chicken coop. The four dogs also protected my books, which I happily kept in a wooden crate with a tight-fitting lid. The combination of container and guards made it impossible for the mice to get in and attack the books. Only one of my books was nibbled on during all my war years on the farm.

Paca had adopted me when I arrived on the farm and never left my side. No bribe from the farmer's wife, who was a jealous woman, could lure him away; the dog responded only to my commands. The farm woman finally gave me the dog and said that I would be able to take him with me at the end of war. She kept her promise. In the meantime I took care of all four dogs, giving special attention to cleaning the fleas and ticks with which they were plagued all summer.

Paca was an alert companion and warned me regularly, signaling danger at every suspicious sign. I don't know how he sensed what threatened my safety, how he knew that for me, danger would primarily take the form of any stranger who would appear in the vicinity, but he could actually hear the sound of menace long before I did. Paca never barked, but just let out a slight growl, signaling to me that there was good reason to watch out. I had not taught him this behavior; I came to believe that it was just his special awareness of and response to my particular need. With his special, slight warning signal, Paca became as invisible as I was.

I often thought about how in wartime, haphazard chance could change the whole pattern of events. At first glance, it certainly seemed that way. Years later I started to believe that there were no random occurrences. Events didn't just happen. There were entire arrays of circumstances which had to exist and fit into what then had the appearance of a predesigned pattern. Those seemingly incidental fragments had to link into each other in their perfect fit.

It was a morning in midsummer. I was inhaling the beauty of the surrounding hills, still languishing in slight fog. The cool air and sumptuous smell of wildflowers were all around when Paca and I started our morning walk up the hill to the spring. It was that kind of day when war and atrocities seemed far distant from what I was doing or even thinking about. Nature was a blessing that provided many of the elements missing from my otherwise starved existence.

On my way back, lugging the heavy water cans, walking slowly as the summer heat was rising, I heard Paca growling. We were still quite far from the road, in a densely wooded area. I knew immediately that he had heard an alarming noise I could not detect. Between the trees and overgrown shrubs, I could barely see the house where the two small children were in hiding. There was a car in front of the house with several men in civilian clothing. I was horrorstruck, knowing full well what was unfolding. Somehow those children had been discovered and the Nazis were taking them away. I felt devastated. There was nothing I could do but stand in the safe distance. I didn't even know if the Nazis were searching all the other houses in the area. Well hidden, in the shade of abundant foliage, I couldn't be seen from the road. I had to wait, to observe, and to be miserable in my passivity. I recognized the small girl's resemblance to the woman who was leading her out of the house. It must have been her mother. She was also carrying the boy, who was hugging her. The girl walked slowly behind them, holding a doll in one hand and a small suitcase in the other, looking back at the farmhouse.

The road was deserted. I couldn't see anyone anywhere. All the windows and shutters of the surrounding houses were closed. The midday heat was still hours away, but no one wanted to witness what was so obviously happening. Another family was being taken to their slaughter. I felt both an overwhelming sorrow for the two small doomed children and fear for my own safety. Confronting these two emotions together made me sit on the ground crying. Paca was licking my tears.

It took me a long time to arrive back at my farm. I explained the delay and my reluctance to move from my hidden spot since I had no way of knowing whether the Nazis were searching any other places. The farmer's wife understood. Later she told me about the rumors concerning what had happened. The Nazis had caught the hidden children's father, and he turned out to be someone important. Then the mother led the authorities to the farm where the children had been left in hiding.

Who am I to say that by that period in the war the mother should have known well enough not to trust any promises made by the obsessive bloodthirsty oppressor? Maybe she hoped and even believed that her hidden children could by some chance remain undetected and stay alive.

Was the circulating story true?

Later, whenever I came near that house where I had seen those two hidden children, who by now were gone, I experienced a recurring pain. I tried many times to feel compassion for their mother, so young and distressed, who had had to make a decision of such magnitude. Deep in my psyche I could never find a way to agree with her decision to lead the murderers to her children's hiding place.

When I was a small child, when life was just starting to become an overwhelming adventure, I couldn't part with my rabbit, and so killed it because I loved it so much. I had to have him beside me all the time. I could not understand. Reality forced me to accept the result. With my growing awareness of how hatred became the big killer in the world, I was haunted by a solemn memory from my childhood—that love could kill as well. Those children were deprived of even the slight chance they might have had if they had been left in hiding.

I have not erased that scene of the two children walking out of the house, from the marginal safety of hiding, into the certainty of doom. I have never forgotten those children, nor have I lost the sadness of their being gone.

at an early age I was taught
to curb my rage accept defeat
get skilled in that field
yield to pressure take the blow accept dismay
try to comprehend the slasher
who has to mend his own despair
and does not care at whom or where
he'll throw his dart to rid himself of venom
I did not build up immunity
to the poison brew cast at me
piled were injuries
but scars formed a firm shield

THE PARTY

S AINT NICHOLAS DAY WAS A MAJOR RELIGIOUS HOLIDAY, or Slava—probably the most important day of the year for Greek Orthodox families, especially those who, for generations, had celebrated Saint Nicholas as their protector. Sveti Nikola, as they called him, was the patron of the family who gave me shelter during the war. He was their Slava. Even in the hungry December of 1943, with food reserves dramatically reduced, Slava was the one day of abundance.

I remembered this from previous years and was looking forward to a generous meal. The greatest delicacy for me was the absolutely essential finale to the meal—the *kolievo*—prepared days in advance. Sprouting wheat kernels would be ground with nuts mixed with honey—and then formed into a dome on a large platter. To prevent the mixture from drying, the luscious mound was covered with fine sugar, and this became the glaze.

My task was to prepare the powdered sugar in a large mortar. The size and scope of the *kolievo* had to be bountiful. No one involved—hosts or guests—wanted to be without enough leftovers from the day of Slava. That was part of the tradition.

I was surprised a couple of days before the Slava, when I was told that I was to go and be with the farmers' Godchild for the day. Verica was my age and her parents had let her invite close friends to a party, not just for the formal traditional visit to offer congratulations. I had met Verica's parents before, when they had come to the farm. Because the two families were closely connected, they knew about my being in hiding. They shared the same Slava, they were Kooms, which meant that someone in each family had been best man in a wedding of the other family. My farmers were godparents to Verica and her infant brother, the latter being the real pride of his middle-aged parents.

I was reassured that I didn't have to be concerned about the guests invited to the party. To everyone there I would simply be introduced as a distant relative working as a farmhand. Slava was just the right time to be kind to people and to allow a young girl who everyone would recognize was isolated have some contact with people her own age. This was to be the explanation for my presence. Anyway, no one would ask me too many questions, because having information could be self-destructive. In times of occupation, everyone learns that lesson fast.

I was too excited to be apprehensive about my safety. Going to a party in the city, meeting and talking to young people after not having had any contact for almost three years with any teenager—I was thrilled. It did occur to me that I might look odd to others. And yet, despite all that time on the farm, alone and lonely, I had been reading and thinking a lot, and so I felt adequate enough to hold a conversation. On the other hand, at seventeen, even in wartime, I was aware that my clothing and shoes would probably be out of place. This was the source of some concern.

Verica's family lived in an affluent neighborhood. She was in the last grade of high school and her friends would be at that same educational and social level that used to be my own before the war. I wondered how out of place I would be at the party—especially the way I looked in 1943. For the last years I had been living in a room adjacent to a chicken coop and pigsty. There was only cold water in the faucets—and even that was not clean enough to drink.

Washing laundry on the farm and then hanging it out in freezing weather had made my hands red and swollen. Chopping wood, also part of my responsibility, had developed my muscles and given me a tan. On occasion, I would have to go to the mill with sacks of grain, where I would climb the ladder with the burden on my back. Slowly pouring the grain into the funnel, I had become a manual laborer.

The farm routine was my way of life. I got used to sitting on the ground or a chunk of wood while tending to the baby chicks. It was my responsibility to keep them warm enough, fed enough, and free of the lice that used to cling to the heads of these newly hatched, vulnerable youngsters. If they were not removed, these parasites would eventually kill the chicks. I had to keep my chickens growing. That was not only an order from the farmer, it became my ambition to keep them healthy. The animals grew attached, surrounding me when I entered the fence, crowding around to be fed and cleaned of the menacing pests.

What at the beginning seemed to me like simply a game developed into relating to the fluffy little birds as beings. I could never eat them later, when they were inevitably consumed by the farmers. Since food was scarce, my attitude was appreciated by my hosts.

I was in a reality completely different from the comfortable one I grew up in. But I was alive and had my tiny space with the bare necessities, such as the winter comforter I had brought from home. It must have been pure chance that I remembered to do that when I came to the farm at the beginning of summer 1941. The comforter saved me from freezing throughout the long and harsh winters that followed. My luxury was a round tin oven the size of a snare drum. Since wood was expensive, I used to gather up spare and sparse branches to heat water for my personal indulgence, a bath. The stove became red-hot quickly and cooled even faster. But it felt good to wash swiftly and crawl into bed clean.

I kept my long hair neatly in braids, which was a complicated task because I had only a wooden comb. Maintaining personal hygiene depended on my ability to improvise. I had to be fast to grab at least one egg from the nest before the farmer could remove them all, and would use the yolk to wash my hair instead of the soap that was like slimy ash.

In spite of being aware of how shabby-looking I was, I jumped at the invitation to the Slava party. I was young and was going to talk to people my age. It was too enticing an opportunity for me to refuse. I was happy to go.

It was a rainy cool day when Verica came to the farm to take me to her home. It was extremely nice on her part to have gone to all that trouble, and I was grateful. I understood what the additional reason for her kindness was. We had not met before and she wanted to get acquainted, since she was also bringing me some of her dresses to try on for the party. Her parents must have told her how I was dressed. I had no way of preparing to partake in any festivity. I was clad in layers of falling-apart pieces of clothing and felt very grateful for Verica's kindness. With an engaging smile, she gave me a dark dress that was obviously too small for her since she was taller than me and with a nicely developed bosom. It was easy to like her. She was straightforward, self-assured in the power of her intellect and femininity. We felt comfortable with each other immediately.

During the long walk to her home we both knew this to be a rare chance to talk intimately, one that might not arise again. Verica was looking forward to talking to me. She knew I was in hiding and thus would not breach her trust. She had a boyfriend and had been sexually involved with him for some time. Despite her self-confidence, she was afraid of becoming pregnant. She told me that her parents and even her closest friend did not suspect her of having sex. If they did, her parents would not have let her out of the house, or else they would have insisted that she get married immediately. Verica and her boyfriend wanted to stay in school and of course avoid a family scandal.

It was a long walk to her house, and it was a long story she had to tell someone. Verica understood my avoiding any contact with men and that self-preservation had blocked my hormonal development. Listening to her anxiety and talking to her about my own personal problems made me feel good. I was an outcast, but ordinary life was flourishing around me. People my age had their time filled with the usual patterns of behavior and desire: school, intrigues, hairdos, and glimpses of fashion. Life created forbidden love and fears of being caught, the thrill of hiding intimacies. There was normal existence out there. War had not completely destroyed nature, and that felt good.

I was certainly in an anticipatory mood upon entering Verica's home. Needless to say, her dress didn't fit me well, as I was slender and flat-chested. Even before I saw them, I knew I looked different from all the other girls. They were well groomed, and I was weathered. Somehow it didn't bother me. Just to be in a room with people my age felt wonderful. Listening to the sound of chatter, not paying attention to the content, was pleasant.

They were all so involved in themselves that I could just as well have been a piece of furniture. It was a somewhat sad reality for me to face, but I tried to convince myself that it was safer than if they'd taken an interest in me as a person. I was in hiding, living an extremely different life. For me this was a short holiday from my gray day-in, day-out existence. I could not talk about that.

The whole apartment was filled with noise and smells of food, pleasantly warm and hospitable. Some guests were dancing. The records were from before the war; I remembered the tunes. I really hoped one of the young men would ask me to dance. I used to be a very good dancer, but no one could know that. Definitely not from the way I was dressed. I probably looked younger or just underdeveloped. Being entirely overlooked by all the young people in the room made me feel so unimportant. Then it hit me—I was just nobody to anyone here.

There were more young men than girls at the party, but even that did not make a difference. It didn't occur to me that I looked so horribly unattractive and that this might have been the reason why none of the young men standing around would consider inviting me to dance. They didn't even glance at me. From the beginning of the war I had tried to hide my developing womanhood carefully. I knew I could become fair game to men around the village and adjacent farms, so I had to protect myself by looking and acting as plain as possible; I didn't want to attract anyone's second look. I must have succeeded beyond expectations. People were dancing and having a good time. I was invisible to all.

A poem of Erich Kästner came to my mind, in which a blind beggar says, "I can not see anyone—therefore I am invisible to everyone." No one was noticing my existence. I was as invisible as the blind man whom the seeing world refuses to notice. I must have smiled at the ridiculous situation I was in. Then a young man stood in front of me. He was much taller than I, but everyone in the room was. A rather deep voice jolted me into reality: "Don't you have a toothbrush? Your teeth are half rotted away."

I thought I'd die of shame. I could not tell this man how my teeth were broken at the very beginning of the occupation. It was one of those incidents. My mother had a ration book which would be used eventually for buying food. She had acquired it through her old birth certificate. I was visiting her and tried to be helpful, running errands for her, such as waiting in line for potatoes. Since I was already in hiding, it was dangerous for me to be in town. But I risked it sometimes, especially at the beginning of the war, just wanting to see my mother and sister—homesick, I suppose.

It just happened. A German soldier was imposing order on the unruly line of angrily waiting citizens. He did it with his rifle butt—and I got it straight in my mouth. He wasn't aware of what he did, which probably saved my life. After all, he might have insisted on taking me to an infirmary. There, for sure, I would have been found out and shot.

My front teeth were broken; I felt the pieces in my mouth. My lips were bleeding; so was my nose, and I wasn't sure if it hadn't been broken as well. My fear that the soldier would notice what had happened was stronger than the pain. I did not cry out. No one around me paid any attention to me, as no one wanted to get involved. I had learned how to stay deeply silent, in spite of pain.

But I was devastated. A fifteen-year-old girl with broken front teeth, in hiding, doing work I didn't even know existed before the war. The people who gave me shelter were not unkind. I respected them for harboring a fugitive, taking that risk, and I never refused the work they expected from me. Somehow I made it back to the farm, explaining, not complaining. I could not go to a dentist, as I did not legally exist. To do so could very well have endangered me and the people who were giving me refuge. Besides, I most definitely did not have the money for any treatment. I knew my teeth had been broken and were slowly crumbling for lack of care and nourishment. My toothbrush had lost its bristles a long time ago and I couldn't replace it. There was nothing I could do about it.

When that young man threw the truth into my face I was shattered—humiliated by a reality I was powerless to alter. He was so crude, possibly just showing off his masculine power. But he was right. I did look horrible, with my front teeth broken in half. At that time in my life, my place was not at anyone's party. I was a person with no identification papers, no home, welcomed only by the dogs and the chickens on the farm. Everyone else was slightly afraid when I appeared. I understood that. Even on the farm it was better if I stayed as invisible as possible. My presence was tolerated, not appreciated.

I was not going to give that young man at the party the satisfaction of seeing me burst into tears. I remember concentrating all my energy on not letting that arrogant man have his ultimate satisfaction by showing how deeply he had hurt me. I maintained my dignity by keeping silent, disregarding his presence, walking slowly past him as if he didn't exist, and walking on out of the room. I had to get out, to find a secluded spot where I could recover my composure. What I did was to hide in the washroom; that was a beautiful place compared to the outhouse I used on the farm. I couldn't cry since that would have been visible when I emerged from my temporary privacy, the short respite where I regained my calm. I had deceived myself into believing there could be a reprieve from the war reality I was locked into. I'd made a mistake by thinking that for at least a couple of hours, I could be a regular teenager. It just wasn't possible.

I thanked Verica for her generosity, her parents for letting me be part of their celebration, and started the long walk back to the farm.

My father's words before we parted two years earlier were: "Do not feel sorry for yourself or someone else. Do something to make a change if you can. Try not to indulge in feelings; we cannot afford them in this time we live in."

I did feel sorry for myself. I was desperate about the insult I had received. All the pain I had suffered thus far, never complaining, was pressing in my chest, turning breathing into a strenuous effort. And there was no one to console me by just listening. This time the pain was deeper than the blow to my face from the German soldier's rifle butt. That had been an accident; I was merely the casualty. Here was a young man who had deliberately hurt and humiliated me. I couldn't cry in the street because it might have attracted attention—the last thing I wanted. I felt as low as I ever did before.

The memory of that long walk from the party to the farm is still sharp in my mind. Tears were burning in my throat. It would have felt so good to at least cry. The last time I had cried was years earlier. I knew then that I wasn't going to cry anymore. There was no place in my reality to feel sorry for myself.

I had last cried when I was leaving the city to walk to the farm for the first time. The German army had just entered Belgrade. Within the city, fires were still smoldering. The air of death was rising out of the many destroyed buildings. Nazi bombers had covered the city with a cloud of Hell. Some parts of town just didn't exist anymore after the onslaught. I was passing through a section that had completely burned to the ground. It used to be part of one of the major streets where Jewish merchants had their shops. It struck me how accurate the aim of the firebombers must have been. This was the most damaged part of the city—the Jewish quarter.

I was afraid to move through the deserted side streets, and had chosen a wide main road where a mass of slowly moving people was heading south. Some had pushcarts piled with belongings that looked like salvage out of the rubble. Those people leaving the city must have lost their homes. And there were the German soldiers, just taking photographs and laughing, not stopping anyone. The river of defeated humanity had created a safe way for me to leave town.

On my first journey to find my hiding place, my load was only a backpack; I was moving faster than the crowd. Some people were sitting on their parcels at the side of the road, exhausted. There was a horse standing very still, almost in the middle of the street. Having been wounded in the leg, the animal could control the pain only by not moving. A broken cart was overturned beside the horse. Mercifully he wasn't tied to it anymore. As a child, I used to ride, so I was drawn to the animal. I started to stroke the horse's forehead, which was completely wet with his sweat. With a wound that had already crusted over, he must have been in agony. Only a tiny rivulet of blood was flowing down his leg. I put my arms around his neck, sobbing. I couldn't recall having cried like that before.

Neither did I know how long I stood there, hugging the wounded horse. He was never going to gallop, trot, or even walk; I could never walk back into my life, the way it had been.

I was crying for myself—sharing sorrow with this doomed animal. There was nothing I could do to ease its pain or my fears for my own safety. Life was ruled by chance. A German soldier approached, drawing his gun. People started to push away from the horse and me and to run. I stroked the horse's trembling head once more and moved away slowly. I couldn't look, and so only heard the shot and the thud of the falling body hitting the ground. Shooting the wounded horse was a matter of noble mercy for the German soldier. Here was my enemy, who would have put a bullet into my head with no pity—I knew that. Maybe even shoot me for the pleasure of killing a Jew. And here was I, feeling gratitude toward that soldier who had spared the animal prolonged suffering.

With those conflicting emotions of gratitude, fear for my own existence, and contempt for the ruthless oppressor, I was moving south, out of the city. I knew that I wasn't going to cry for myself again. Walking the long road back to the farm after the party made me aware of how immensely different my life had become. That first walk to the farm seemed not like years but decades ago. As time passed, I wondered whether there was any other life than the one I was experiencing. Imagining an existence less bleak than my backbreaking daily routine had become more and more elusive. The Slava party I had just left some hours ago had given me a glimpse, as through an open window, into a different life. But I was on the outside and only allowed to look in. There was no place for me at any party.

On this seemingly endless walk toward my hiding place, I wished I could have had a horse on the road to hug and let my tears flow freely.

The road was empty and my eyes were dry.

dark bats against dim dawn
flutter their wings and fly
there are no songs at night
soft shy cries consumed by daybreak

TRAPPED

ANIMALS HAD SOMETHING of an exhilarating effect on me. It must have been fear—that fascinating upsurge of tension that made me alert and could arouse my whole being. As a small child I could not have explained why I was seeking an agitation bordering on danger. In spite of my fear, however, I actually enjoyed the presence of animals. At times I even relished the presence of those that most people detest, such as bats and rats.

Bats were funny, unusual-looking beasts, hanging upside down when other creatures' heads pointed in the other direction. As a child, when I learned they were mammals just like us, I tried the bat's position a couple of times. While lying on the sofa, I would let my head hang down; it was very uncomfortable. I also liked to watch bats flying at dusk. I still do.

My first introduction to a rat was, needless to say, frightening. It happened at a time when I was barely accepted by the bigger kids in our building complex. No one wanted to include me in the games they played, all of which took place in the apartments' large courtyard. In vain I tried to become part of the group.

An ornate staircase led to the second-floor apartments, and there was a terrace surrounding the yard. None of the bigger children used those wide and imposing stairs; instead, they preferred the ones on the opposite side, called the back of the house. These were dark, narrow, enclosed, and, due to their steep steps, uncomfortable to climb. They were also filled with the odors of decay drifting out of the shaft that had been built for the disposal of the garbage.

The foul air must have intensified the atmosphere, shrouding the place with mystery. A window on the second floor, encased by closely set bars that only added to the ominous atmosphere, was the only place where fresh air could enter. A large iron door on the ground floor, formidable in its own right, was where the refuse was collected. This was the place where the bigger children promised to show me what they called "the Devil."

I had not been raised with fears of the devil, of hell and damnation. I was taught about evil in more general terms. Evil was doing harm to someone, so it wasn't done. One of the joys in my childhood lay in accepting such simple explanations. For me, images of the devil simply represented the artist's freedom to paint them, so many examples of which I found in art books in the family library.

My greatest learning experience occurred in later years when I realized the terrible danger that confronts children when they are exposed to deceptive images. Most of my childhood conceptions were based on the prejudices and superstitions handed down to me by adults. That which truly represented the basic evil that resides within us and without, I had to learn from being alone, without guidance.

When I was very young, the older kids in our apartment house didn't want to play with me. They played scary games about a "Devil" hidden somewhere on the back stairs, inside the foul-smelling garbage dump. One day I was asked to join the group of kids going up the back stairs. I knew then that this was going to be my encounter with the Devil. It was my first lesson in how to cope with fear and not show it. I so badly wanted to win the approval and acceptance of the bigger children. So I was all too willing to go through the initiation rite ordered by them; I would confront that which even they were afraid of.

The confrontation with the Devil remained clear in my mind for years afterward. Like a musical theme with which a tune begins, and which later reappears in variations, that childhood event shaped many decisions I made later in my life.

The group of children started up the back stairs. I knew I was being watched. If I had cried, I would have been sent away. As I steadied myself, I found myself looking down from the upper window into an abysmal shaft filled with decaying food and a foul smell. Our garbage dump.

There it was. The dreaded Devil was sitting on top of the rotting pile, gorging itself. It turned out to be a very big dark rat. At that instant, I expected the rat to turn into a large winged monster, lifting itself out of the trash, reaching with its claws to catch one of us, and of course, it had to be me, being the smallest.

Nothing happened. There was the rat, looking up with intensity, reacting to our intrusion, and it was in a feeding frenzy. I don't remember how long we were there. The rat was eating for a while and then stopped. It was looking up at us and I realized why. The kids were bringing food and throwing it down, feeding the rat, and of course the animal was waiting for each tidbit as it landed near it. I think the logic behind their actions was that if the animal were fed enough, it would become enormously fat and wouldn't be able to run away. The end result would be that the man who collected the garbage would kill it.

This really was a poor devil—being trapped to be killed. I couldn't articulate what was wrong with the children's plan, but I felt there was something evil in it.

I hadn't yet started school, and so during morning hours there wasn't much for me to do, no one to play with. I started to visit the rat. It probably didn't take long for me to become friendly with the animal, especially once it recognized my voice—when I talked to it, it looked up while sitting still. Maybe we both got used to not feeling afraid of each other anymore.

Then it somehow became clear to me that the bigger children were planning something cruel for this animal. It had not done them any harm, yet they wanted it killed.

I don't believe I could have had any liking for the rodent, but I wanted to free it before the garbage men could hit it with the big shovels they used to clean up the mess. It was probably the first time in my life that I had an idea and followed it through.

My plan made me feel proud; I was aware of that at the time. Here's how it went: The garbage was thrown through the window, through its rusty bars and broken glass. It was too hard for me to open the handle, but I was sure that there had to be a way to set the animal free. I wasn't strong enough to move anything like a ladder or to lower it into the shaft. The only idea I could come up with was to break off a large branch from my grandmother's geranium plant and throw the abundant offshoot down into the garbage dump and then leave the window open for the rat's escape. The branch, which unfortunately only reached half the distance to the window, didn't do the trick and gave rise to a new concern. I was afraid to watch and see whether the rat was going to climb the branch and escape. At any rate, I hoped to have spoiled the deadly plan of the bigger children. At the very least, it was satisfying for me to have acted alone.

A great uproar broke out when the bigger children came home from school and found that the rat was gone. They were all so excited about the power of the Devil who had escaped that they completely disregarded me as a possible instrument in the matter. Though of course I was happy about my success, I was also afraid of being found out. I had tried so hard to be included in their games and they had kept me out. After the rat escaped, I didn't care any more whether they would or would not accept me. They did.

In all our lives there are years and events that drift into oblivion. Then something triggers our memory. It can be a sight, a sound, or smell, and we slip into a long-forgotten crevice of our experience from the past. A familiar circumstance, if not identical, then at least associative, and out of it comes the memory of a situation one has seemingly forgotten.

World War II reached my hometown about ten years after my childhood experience with the trapped rat. In the meantime my life had changed in various ways. I had started middle school and we had left the apartment building and had moved into our own house. Then in 1940, just one year before our part of Europe was overrun by the invading Nazi forces, we moved to Belgrade.

I knew about the occupied places, where the Nazis were setting human achievements on a backward course and were mercilessly killing innocent people. War was imminent, closing in on us. I myself was taking part in student demonstrations, where we marched with slogans like "Better death than slavery." I was terrified.

I knew history quite well, all of it from books about heroic battles of the past, all with their romantic embellishments. The writing represented those whose voices were silenced forever. The closer we moved toward the impending onslaught, the more frightened I grew. I did not want to die. I wanted to have a life—to grow up, to grow old.

After the merciless bombing of a defenseless population, the Nazi occupation followed. As Jews, we were immediately persecuted and hunted down by the Nazis and then executed when we were caught. It was during this siege that I remembered my childhood experience with the trapped rat. Though the past can feel as unreal as the future, that memory seemed to be warning me that if I wanted to stay alive I had to escape. Years ago I had opened a barred window for an animal so that it could go free. With that image in mind, I took my chances and left what represented my only source of security, my home and parents.

And there was someone with enough courage to open a door for me, someone to offer me shelter from the hunters, those predators who were perpetually devoted to driving us Jews into extinction.

My recollection now, of how I felt at that particular time in my life, is only fragmented. In the years of war, life didn't have much substance and reflection; it consisted mostly of fears and needs. And that shadowy existence lasted throughout the Nazi occupation. At times, however, there were islands of clarity that became etched into my memory with minute details.

Nowadays this state is called suspended animation. I find it a fair description. One feels as though one is hanging in the air, while elements around us are in turmoil. At those times I would identify with bats, who try to survive in the invisible existence of darkness, hiding and silent. The Nazi era killed 6 million Jews. It maimed us survivors for life.

mine is a world
inhabited by loving ghosts
gone for real
I will not let them wither to dust
after being robbed of dignity banned and bared
their naked life was stolen
in atrocious arrogance
hence I carry the memory
of their past churning cherished life
and tender warmth they thrust upon me
to make me last

SPIRITS

I REMEMBER WHEN I FIRST SAW the photographs of the delicate transparent cloths with their strange inscriptions. Tied to a long pole, they looked like banners, fluttering in the wind. In the background of the photographs were huge mountain peaks, shrouded in mist, forbidding, their sharp edges of rock and ice unattainable. The images seemed mysterious and beautiful and captivated me for life.

At that time, when I was about twelve, I was very much involved with ghosts. The book of photographs was about Buddhist monks in Tibet. The accompanying text explained that the monks were sending messages to spirits. The inhabitants of these magnificent mountains regularly climbed their prohibitive windy peaks, tying their inscribed banners, trusting them to the wind, talking to their dead.

That of course was long ago. At times, it seems to me it was many lives ago. If I give way to fancies, I could say that my life now must be one that was reincarnated. It really is so different; centuries might have passed since I died and I was not aware of it. So I just lived on and on.

That era of long-ago events and of all the people close to me had all vanished from my life. It would have been easier for me to adjust to loss if, like the Buddhist monks, I could have sent messages carried by the wind to those I loved and who were killed.

Later on, life's circumstances piled up, one upon the other, like bodies in mass graves. I never said good-bye to any one of my loved ones lost in the war.

I was born in the flatlands, a geological depression, the bottom of a vanished lake. Because of this formation and my sense of it, there is an enormous distance upward from where my mind was formed to the peaks where the Buddhists dwell.

My home was in Novi Sad, a small town on the Danube in the northern part of Yugoslavia. When the war started for us in 1941, the life we had been used to completely disintegrated. At first, the period was characterized by unrestrained dehumanization, carried out by the Nazi occupying power. Then, after depriving us Jews of our dignity, the next step became cold-blooded murder.

Postwartime, after 1945, was an intermission in our history of grand-scale killings. People here and there disappeared, but it was done quietly, and as a group, we Jews were not the main targets any more. We were now living under a different dictatorship.

It was an unfortunate place I had been born in. Within a short time, the dormant animosity of people in the region erupted again. It seems so easy to incite hatred, fighting, and murder.

From time to time during decades past, I wished I could have sent messages, just like the Buddhist monks, to at least one of my ghosts. Of all the people killed in the war, the one I missed most was my sister.

There are many spirits I feel connected to from that time, and years have not erased the bond. The link with them is deeply embedded in my brain. I did not say how I felt to most of those who vanished, and I could have done so when they were still alive. I did not reveal how much I loved them; unsaid words do not disappear, people do.

For a long time I hoped the people I lost would reappear. Especially my sister, with whom I had a close relationship. Although she was five years older than I, she never treated me as someone who was less mature than herself. I could have told her how much that respect meant to me. There was so much more I would have liked to have talked to her about when I saw her last, but didn't. At that time she seemed so happy, and happiness was so unusual then, and all that mattered. She had on her best dress and her wavy hair was neatly brushed. She was very beautiful and I was so pleased to see her smiling.

Next time I came to visit, she was not in the apartment. I knew she was dead. Neither then nor later on, when I could make inquiries, did anyone clarify what had happened.

"She will get in touch with you," they told me at the partisan headquarters. That was all the information I ever received.

Throughout long periods of passing time, the lost opportunity to talk to my sister, especially to tell her how much I loved her, rested like a heavy load on me. I missed her badly. Years after she was gone and my hopes for her return had dwindled, the feeling that overtook me was remorse. I felt that I had failed to prevent her from being killed. In some unreal way I believed she might have stayed alive if I just had talked to her once more before we parted.

Needless to say, my feelings weren't rational then or ever since. Whatever we would have talked about, nothing could have changed events. Atrocities of the war were advancing like molten lava, devouring everything in its way.

Fanciful longing for my sister throughout my life has created many nonspoken dialogues within me. They must have become part of purging myself for being alive after she became one of the 6 million killed. I could never really comprehend the monstrosity of the numbers and statistics of that mass killing.

Obliterating the individual, honoring the sanctity of orderly classification, listing numbers, percentages—that may be the only way we can cope with the stockpiling of cataclysmic events.

It may very well be that when I thought about what I possibly could have told my sister, I was hoping to avoid facing those dreams she had shared with me. For now there was only reality to be dealt with. Of course, at that time I was not mature enough to have made such a statement. Those comforting and yet guilt-laden thoughts came years later.

During the war, my body as well as my brain was starved. I did not have the capacity for much logical or rational thinking. My actions were probably activated by reflexes alone: to run, to escape. It took me years to accept the fact that those animal instincts and behavior were part of me. It was embarrassing to admit to myself that I was a coward, that I would avoid confrontations, that I was ready to hide in order to stay alive.

So very few Jews survived the initial onslaught of the Nazi occupation when, following the order to do so, everyone obediently went to register. All those Jews who registered were killed soon after.

The place of that mass murder, which was called the fairgrounds of Zemun, was across the river Danube on the bank opposite the city of Belgrade. Before the war, Zemun had been designated as a place for fun, a site where amusement parks would be set up. What a cynical plan of the Nazis to choose that location for carrying out their atrocities.

When it became known that a horrifying mass murder was taking place just across the river, it was, of course, too late. All the Jews who were rounded up in Belgrade and its surrounding areas were dead. According to the rumors that circulated, there was a convoy of large gray trucks, supposedly for transport. Then one day the trucks were gone. So was every Jew who had been brought to the fairgrounds of Zemun. No one ever came back.

There were no gladiators and lions. In the ancient Roman circus, people condemned to death for the spectators' amusement at least had the chance to try and fight the beasts. But these were modern times. The primitive urge to kill and enjoy the show had undergone a metamorphosis, generating a new culture. Only the location carried the association of entertainment from the world of antiquity. The beasts we faced could not be fought, especially since they came in a different lethal form: gas pumped into sealed metal containers in which the victims were enclosed. This beastliness had a purpose: to measure the amount and effectiveness of a new gas that was later used in the concentration camps. It was proven a success in Zemun, the prewar fairground.

As soon as the Nazi occupation began, there was only a slim chance that one could remain undetected during the persistent searching for hidden Jews. My family did not obey the order to register. We decided to take the risk of being caught and immediately killed. What we did not know then was that to obey would have meant death anyway. The deception to round up people and make them silently enter a slaughterhouse was appalling.

My sister's fiancé married her after the war had started, and it became obvious that this improvised idea represented only a meager chance for survival. My sister's fiancé was a Serbian and had been a government employee prior to the war. During the Nazi occupation and according to their laws, he was forbidden to do what he did. Besides love, his action took courage.

He found a Greek Orthodox priest who was willing to go against the restrictions and act on their behalf, and so the marriage certificate he made out predated the beginning of war. It was a risky and expensive act.

Out of concerns for my brother-in-law's safety, the marriage was kept secret. Only his closest friend, who served as the witness, knew about it. His family was not to be trusted. As a result of the secrecy, my sister was treated by her husband's family as an unwanted concubine, representing only danger. His family's attitude grew increasingly hostile, and this, in the long run, had a damaging effect on the young couple's relationship. As much as she tried to understand his family's fears about the dangerous involvement they all shared and nobody wanted, the constant insults took their toll. Her husband did not or could not stop the nasty remarks his family made.

The document citing my sister's marriage to a non-Jew offered some security so long as she didn't have to show it to officials. The strict legality of that marriage would have been a necessary precaution if the family had contested it. That was all my sister had, as a young woman, from the man she loved and we all trusted.

My brother-in-law did show his devotion to my sister by finding me a hiding place on a farm. I could not have done it without him, and I was grateful. The farmers were ready to take me in exchange both for the work I was to do for them and for some additional compensation.

I appreciated the daring of the farmers—to spite the Nazis and hide a Jew. And so I worked very hard and never refused any task; I fulfilled my part of the deal as well as they did.

My mother had not been born Jewish. She had converted, choosing to change her religion. Father, who had met her during World War I, regretted her decision to become a Jew, especially twenty years later, when anti-Semitism had exploded and expanded with no limits.

Before the war, my sister and I, still children, inquired why Mother had chosen to convert to Judaism. My sister and I were raised as Jews; there was no doubt in our minds where we belonged. We just wanted an explanation, as it seemed somewhat strange to us that Mother had wished to join a minority that was not just disliked but hated almost everywhere. She had been born to a more privileged group in the society we lived in.

Mother explained that as a young girl she went to confession regularly, but the priest she had trusted since childhood had taken advantage of her trust, and tried to seduce her; by converting, she was renouncing an institution that had not only misused her spiritual needs but had shattered her beliefs as well. There was no way, she concluded, that she could stay with people with no moral values. In Judaism she found she was treated with integrity as a person. Even during the war, she claimed to have made the right decision. I have always admired my mother's steadfastness.

It must have been difficult for Father to leave us, though we understood; his going away gave us a better chance to blend in to the precarious existence of hiding. He couldn't protect us anymore. On the contrary, his presence became compromising for us, he said, and we all knew he was right.

There had been no declaration of war, but Belgrade was relentlessly hit by waves of heavy bombardments. After a couple of hours, it seemed that the whole city was going to be destroyed. The Jewish quarter was completely burned to the ground. The Germans knew the targets they wanted to hit and did.

We were in a basement that was not built to be an air raid shelter; none of the residential buildings had one. The ground was shaking from the explosions. I remember the coarse tweed of Father's jacket when, filled with terror, I put my cheek against his chest. He was a meticulous dresser, with the scent of lavender and tobacco around him.

My upbringing did not encourage the seeking of consolation in my father's embrace. Even under stressful circumstances, it was not the usually expected behavior. But he must have seen how terribly frightened I was of being buried in the building. He took me out of the cellar while the air raid was still on.

Father had been a soldier in the First World War; I felt confident leaving the flimsy shelter with him and was relieved to see the sky. At fifteen one is not really afraid to die. Being trapped under a collapsed building was what I dreaded.

The street in front of the house was a gaping smoldering crater when we came up from the cellar. The house across from ours didn't exist any more. It was leveled to the ground. No one could have survived that destruction.

It was then that Father told me: "Don't feel sorry for people you cannot help. Most of all, do not feel sorry for yourself." I knew instantly that what he said was important, yet the meaning grew clear only with time and experience. I never told him how much I was going to miss him, because I didn't know that before he left. This was April 1941 and I was a teenager, without ever having experienced what that blooming time of life is about. We all had to make quick and mature decisions and hope they were the right ones.

Grandmother still lived in Novi Sad, our former hometown. Once Yugoslavia collapsed, and the Nazi occupation of Serbia was in place, Novi Sad was annexed to Hungary. Now that the Hungarian territory was regained through German intervention, it represented an option for survival, and so Father decided to go there and try to find shelter for himself and his mother. Being a rather well known amateur musician, my father had organized many charity musical events between the wars to gain support for Hungarian minority groups. This experience made him confident that his Hungarian friends would protect him and Grandmother. Father was right; he did have a short respite until he was caught by the Nazis' last roundup of Jews at the end of the war. Father and Grandmother perished at Auschwitz.

Mother managed to stay in Belgrade; with her non-Jewish birth certificate, she was able to acquire identification papers. She took a small apartment with my sister. I was on the farm. On rare occasions I would visit them, but it was always hazardous to go into town. If I had been stopped and then asked for identification papers, I knew I would have to run and risk being shot in the back. This probability became one of my nightmares, lasting for decades, long after the war had ended.

Running, that futile activity that is so common in dreams, when one's limbs feel like lead and don't obey our desperate need to escape from a menacing situation. When I had those dreams, they always ended with a piercing pain in my back—and I would wake up drenched in cold sweat.

During one of my visits, my sister confided in me what was going on between her and her husband. He was twenty years older than she and enjoyed the patriarchal privileges of the Balkan male. It took a while for him to admit that he had lost all the funds entrusted to him by my mother and sister. Because money and the family jewelry could not have been put in a bank, all our liquid assets had been given to my sister's husband for safekeeping. But when, after some time, he was no longer supplying his wife and mother-in-law with the funds they needed to live, it became clear that something was terribly wrong. Finally, he had to admit that the money had been lost in card games, and he had no way of replacing it. This was a terrible blow to his pride.

This irresponsibility, coupled with his false pride, doomed my sister's relationship with him. She became the constant target for his frustrations and was punished accordingly. It took some time for her to realize that the insults she was showered with were the result of his shame. What followed was the logical consequence of her realization—a great love turned into grave disappointment and mistrust. It ended in detachment. The damage was irrevocable. All the admiration my sister had felt for him before he abused our complete trust was gone. It also left her and Mother with no means.

I soon learned that as a result of all this, my sister completely abandoned whatever feeling she might once have had for her husband. She admitted to me that she could just as well read the newspaper while he was making love to her. I remember her saying that. It shocked me deeply. I never forgot it.

And yet it didn't surprise me when she told me later about having an abortion. When she had told her husband about her pregnancy, he just let her know it would be all right; since his sister would adopt and take care of the baby, there was no problem. In saying this to her, he had shown blatant and total indifference to the mother of his child. Legally, he could have taken away my sister's child. She had an abortion.

After that, there was no longer any intimacy between them. My sister refused to be receptive to his occasional needs. Then she found part-time work where she wasn't asked for identification papers.

In that third year of war, it was an altogether bleak existence. I never really wanted to reconstruct that perilous period. I could not then nor after half a century think of any redeeming feature to lighten up that somber reality. We were on the dark side of life where even shadows didn't have a brightened outline. At times, one sees around the darkest space.

War had drained all our resources and emotions. Even my fears were gone. Life became quite meaningless. There was no more consolation that at some point the war was going to be over and I might be alive and start my adulthood. I didn't want to be a grown woman. What had happened to my sister had a long-lasting influence upon my own development. Those indeed were desperate times.

When we met some months later, my sister told me that she was in love again. She looked very happy, and that made me happy as well. It was the last time I saw her. She had a radiating halo surrounding her, symbolizing a short gleam of light for her before she was killed. She was pregnant at that time and by the man she was in love with.

When she was gone, never to return, there was no mourning because it was much easier to hope. I hoped for her return for some time. Mother hoped for the rest of her life.

Years of sorrow followed me after I finally accepted that there would never be any more news about my sister. The fighting partisan forces did not provide lists, and I could not get any information.

I would have loved to have possessed the firm Buddhist faith and conviction to trust messages from the mountaintops that would be carried by the winds for my sister.

I still would.

waiting in anterooms
exuding harsh light
where pending uncertainty lurks
waiting under the cloak of night
sheltered from the glare of reality
I do not know which I prefer

MATHILDA'S STORY

*The testimony of my most missed friend. No one was there
to listen, to record, or to remember, except me.*

"WHAT IS YOUR NAME?"

I didn't want to answer. I had always dreaded that question. All
my life, stating my name had produced something painful, in a way
degrading. During the war it was life-threatening.

If only my name had not been Mathilda Cohen, I might have
had a chance to escape deportation in the first place. These were the
thoughts that followed me through the horrifying train journey
that led to what I could never talk about even after the war.

Right now I cannot allow myself that memory. The horrendous
ordeal was half a century ago. Yet it has never left me. My memories are like gargoyles, all around and within, staring at me with
their motionless stony glares.

"What is your name?" The question was repeated a couple of
times. Impatience was already overtaking the voice.

"Mathilda." I said it reluctantly. Even now, I resent saying that
name. As a child, I believed that my parents had inflicted a handi-
cap on me by choosing that name. They used to call me Tellee,
stretching the last vowel until it sounded like a lament. Whenever I
remember my childhood, I feel deep dissatisfaction with, even a
grudge toward, my parents. Then sadness hits me, because they are
gone. I feel guilty for having survived the war. When that emotion
ebbs, the resentment I felt as a child returns. In a way, my parents
embarrassed me. Will I ever get rid of this childhood discontent
about my parents? So many grown-ups carry these useless burdens
through life.

If I try to picture my parents as I saw them last, they were about the age I am now. Mother is an aging, overweight matron, dressed in shapeless black gowns with frills enhancing her opulence, and a brooch just below her double chin. And I wanted my mother to be glamorous, slender and well dressed and, of course, young.

My parents were so much older than what society at that time accepted as an appropriate childbearing age; my sister's children were older than I. They laughed, calling me "Auntie."

I was told by our household maids that it was indecent for older people to have a baby. At that time, I didn't understand what they meant, so I felt as if I might have done something wrong.

My mother seemed confused in her dealings with me; it must have been difficult for her to conceive that she still did conceive. Father's pride when I was very small changed later on when times became more threatening. He became tired and morose. Poor man, he must have been worried and frightened with the responsibility of raising a child at his age, in such a politically turbulent time.

Everyone around me was old; the whole town was old, out of the vanished era of the Austro-Hungarian Empire. All the relatives who came to visit seemed as though they had materialized from another time and place. Always complaining with great gusto about some malady, fatigued, I suppose, from just talking constantly about where it hurt at the moment.

My parents must have been very generous to have let all those complaining relatives stay at our house when they visited the neighboring mud spa. Drinking the sour-smelling mineral water was supposed to heal a wide array of disorders. The cures seemed as endless to me as the number of relatives suffering from their afflictions. Such bores, and I had to be quiet and polite. What I especially hated was that I had to kiss all those flabby cheeks that smelled of face powder and mothballs.

As a small child, I had no playmates, so I invented them. It was a solitary game, but with no disappointments. My imaginary friend was Fredericka. I loved that name. My Fredericka was dainty and slender, with willowy blond hair and elegantly dressed in velvet and lace.

The maids who worked in the house frequently took me to the movies, and this is where I must have gotten the image that became so important to me. I could picture myself being Fredericka, who would sing popular songs and accompany herself on the piano. I would have loved to play music like that and to have had an audience applaud. At times, Fredericka would wear glittering ice-skating outfits, and she would pirouette on the ice, her skirt whirling around her. I had seen this image in movies, and so inspired, I would have loved to have known how to waltz on ice.

I had a wooden horse. Even when it obviously became too small for me, I didn't want to part with it. It would squeal under my weight. Yet when I was sitting on it, I was Fredericka, wearing riding breeches and boots and of course I had a whip with which I could urge my stallion into a gallop beside the ocean. I could practically feel the wind from the water blowing through my hair, the spray of the waves covering my face. I could actually hear the big surf. How I loved those daydreams.

We had never traveled to the seashore. There was just that small lake adjacent to our town. People who visited wallowed in its mud and believed themselves to be cured of whatever ailment.

My pain started when I entered first grade. I would have enjoyed it so much if I could have said: "My name is Fredericka." But there I was, Mathilda, overweight, taller than anyone in the class, a lot of a little girl, with big feet. My classmates called me "Chubby Tellee."

I found myself left out of the group of chattering, giggling schoolmates, so I immersed myself in fancies. As we all grew older, the dreams changed, of course.

By then, Fredericka was singing with a husky voice; her hair would cover her lean face, and she would have a long cigarette holder in her hand. Thin blue smoke spiraling in the light. No one in my class could match that fantasy figure. The velvet and lace dresses were replaced by revealing gowns of silky shiny materials, clinging to the body, with a slit reaching above the knee. A spotlight would follow Fredericka's slim figure within a smoke-filled room. My childhood fancies—there is little else I care to remember from my childhood.

I had no idea how much time had passed since the nurse had asked my name; I had such an urge to say: "My name is Freder—icka." Of course, Fredericka would know how to cope with the information I had been given only a short time ago.

The nurse was pounding the keyboard and the machine started registering me. I am becoming part of a program. I am not Freder-icka, I am even not Mathilda. I am just a code number that will soon be part of a statistic. Number so-and-so reacted favorably to this or that treatment or just died. I feel so defeated. Cancer, undetected for too long, the examining physician had said. Neglected malig-nancy, such a widespread disease nowadays. Fredericka would have gotten an extraordinary illness, one that would have made medical history and been recorded in journals all over the world. I still have my self-indulgent fantasy within reach. What a comfort.

I know I'm smiling, amused with my self-deception, and the nurse is alarmed by now. In the oncology department patients do not smile, especially when they are told to put their affairs in order. She is probably writing down that I am mentally disturbed as well, manifesting odd reactions. I am smiling, yet I want to cry. I don't want to be Mathilda who has cancer. I don't want to die. Maybe I can still escape as I did a long time ago. "Please listen carefully to my questions and give me as much information about yourself as possible. It will make our working together easier in the future."

"I don't have any future!" I feel like screaming.

I am angry at the nurse for asking personal questions. I can give her information about myself that this good woman has never read about. This is her work. She is trying to be helpful. It must be so difficult working with terminally ill people. I am wrong to take out my exasperation on her.

She isn't interested in the part of my life I so carefully kept under wraps for decades. As a matter of fact, no one ever asked me about that time. Years ago, a few people showed some interest: How was it, being deported to the concentration camp at Auschwitz, and what happened there? But when I would start to tell my story, I was asked to stop because it was too painful for them to have to lis-ten to it. Strangely, I wasn't asked how painful those experiences were for me. The less sensitive of the inquisitive just stopped paying attention. I could detect that by the way they looked around and didn't react at all or when they said in an absent way: "How interesting."

I will not burden this woman, with her starched uniform and matching face, with my distant past. I knew there was something wrong with me for some time, and didn't want to face it. Like so many other things in my life, I was always ready to avoid reality; this was my technique for coping with defeat.

"I need some time, maybe half an hour, just to get my bearings, to be silent."

"Of course; take the room across the corridor. It's quiet in there. Would you like a sedative? Since all the tests are done for the time being, I can give you medication so you'll relax and be more at ease."

"Thank you; the room across the corridor will do. I don't want any medication; I want a clear mind."

I am not taking this well. How can I? I want to run, escape. I might still find a way. Right now, my escape route is as far as the room across the passage. Close the door and hide, just as I did for decades, hiding from the truth I couldn't face.

Right now, anything would do. Just get away from the nurse— her watchful stare and questions. Run from unbearable reality. A long time ago, I did it.

Maybe I still can do the impossible. Generate enough power and go against all odds. Strength born out of the fear of dying. I remember well. Fear is so much stronger than pain. I learned that lesson when we arrived at the concentration camp. I was immediately separated from my parents. Barely eleven at that time, I was in panic and pain. I never saw my parents again; I am the only one of my whole family who survived.

Instead of being thrown into the gas chamber, I had been chosen to work on a farm. Only tall, heavyset girls who looked physically strong were selected for work. It was the first real break that came from being Mathilda. The peasant woman I was sent to was angry when I arrived. She said she wanted a man to work on the farm, not a Jewish girl. I tried to work very hard to please her. She hated me deeply.

My life depended entirely on the whims of that unfriendly peasant woman, always irritated, shouting, and angry. Maybe she was as frightened as I was of the war and also of dying. Only she had a gun and carried it all the time. As she grew more and more hostile toward me, I knew that something was going on. There were frightened German-speaking refugees coming from the East with rumors of advancing armies that had already reached German soil.

I knew the peasant woman was going to kill me soon. She would not allow me to talk about what I had seen in the concentration camp. She wouldn't let me report to those liberating armies who were on the way, to tell them the facts about her insulting and abusing me whenever she pleased. I couldn't stand her handling me with her large heavy hands. But I was too scared to say anything, even to her.

She watched me all the time, yet one day, without any preparation, I just ran. Fast and for a long time, straight into the woods. I ran until I couldn't move anymore—and didn't care if I lived or died.

I never knew how long or how far I had run until I joined a group of other escaped prisoners. It all became a haze of starvation and cold. All of us were groping aimlessly through a frozen timeless forest, hungry and needy. There were occasional encounters, when some of the men penetrated my body, but none of them provided me with any warmth or closeness. I knew that soon I wouldn't want to get up from the hard ground after one of those tormenting experiences. It seemed a good trade-off: giving up the consciousness of facing this life for the comfort of oblivion.

What I do remember so sharply from those torments was that I tried to turn to the gratifying childhood fantasies that had helped me overcome mistreatment before. What would Fredericka have done in a situation that I, Mathilda, couldn't figure out how to transform? Fredericka, the dainty but strong, worldly, inventive adventuress?

Fredericka would not have been abused in such a way. She might have been raped because she was beautiful, but those men would somehow have been kinder to her. They might have stayed beside her. They might have given her some food. That fantasy of food was the indulgence I was holding on to at the beginning. Later there was just torture.

I was helpless. Curled up on the ground in my cold misery, completely abused. There was no space left for fantasy. It was real life, and if I had given up, it would have been the end. One was supposed to feel warm before dying from freezing. It could have been an easy death. I, Mathilda, was on my own. If I wanted to stay alive, I'd have to get up and walk away and not give in to the illusion of feeling warm. I did get up, over and over again, after being indiscriminately injured.

These episodes are of course in the distant past. My present struggle is taking place many decades and disappointments later. Yet it feels so like that other defeat, when my body had endured being raped during the war. Can I get up and walk away again? Can I stay alive as in the past? Or am I deceiving myself as I have learned to do?

After my escape from the farm, though I was on the road and free, I found the way so painfully degrading; those men who had humiliated a Jew were not even the enemy. They were fellow mistreated prisoners who had escaped, just as I had.

When I finally made it back to my hometown, I was looked upon with great suspicion. I was told: "The best were killed in the war." I have heard that since, so many times.

"And how did you stay alive?"

What a price to pay for surviving. A shattered self-image for the rest of my days. I will not think now about my defeats. I have to get up, take my chances, and fight my way through, wherever it will take me. I, Mathilda, did stay alive, but did I really get to know what life is? I never came to any understanding about how I lived during all those years passing through me, leaving me more injuries than beautiful memories. To a great extent I used to retreat from the present, from the sense that it was the only time that exists for us. Instead, because of my fears of pain, I opened the door to let in another cluster—of daydreams. Scared to be scarred.

On the other hand, I might not have survived without my fantasies. Fredericka never really died in my mind; I didn't bury her in the snow when I escaped through the winter forest. She is still accompanying me whenever I am overcome by fear or loneliness—like right now.

I have given in to external powers most of my life, and so have compromised in everything, from the trivial to the vitally important. I've always complied with other people and with outer forces. I wish I had fought and stood my ground and not accepted what life and people let me have. Enduring frightening experiences does not make one less sensitive. It just leaves one more and more drained from the inside, until what is left is but an outer shell—a husk devoid of joyful substance filled with exposed nerve endings.

I thought, somehow, that my own decisions were not valid. There was just no one for me to even ask for advice or approval about decisions I had to make. I've let events happen to me because I didn't dare to confront them in opposition. It was a mistake. What a short sentence, but this is my whole life.

I know that I'm going through a retrospective journey. That is all I might have left—to revisit my emotional and physical pains. It is so distressing to think about defeat now. The austere hospital surrounding me is overwhelming. This bitter reality of having cancer, of being terminally ill, feels like looking into a blinding light. The truth is that my blindness was merely self-deception for so many years. I never came to terms with my own basic needs. Fears of rejection have ruled my whole life.

During the war, I even tried to please the farmer woman, that horrendous abusive enemy. By the same token, I have never expressed my deep anger for being raped and later, for so often having been degraded in so many ways. The fear of being excluded has kept me quiet. For many years, silence had been my best ally. I preserved it with great care; I reveled in it. It meant safety. Now I realize that it has turned against me, become my adversary. A slow-growing, malignant silence.

Just a short while ago I asked the nurse for a shelter to be silent in and again I am closing a door and want to hide. Can I possibly change my behavior now? Can I stop hiding? Can I dare to face the part of me I have always carefully concealed? Even when the war ended, I still remained in silent hiding.

Some of my friends who survived the horrors and made the journey home later committed suicide. I never suspected how isolated from life they must have been. I should have confessed my own loneliness to them. Maybe I could have helped them overcome their separation from life, the deep hurt of feeling rejected, of being outcast from people around them.

We who had survived the horrifying slaughter were not wanted when we came back. Our presence reminded people of their own deeds during the war: active in helping to put us away or passive in looking the other way while we were annihilated.

After the journey home that was never home again, I didn't kill myself in an instant stroke, as my friends did. I let my hidden death wish take over slowly. I just didn't take care when the first signs started to warn me that there was something wrong. Maybe I still have some time left to live. I believe that I'm more alive right now than I have been for many years. All my life I dreamed about the vigor and courage Fredericka would have shown in defeat. I realize that in the past, I, Mathilda, have conquered so many of the devastating events happening to me. Without realizing it before, I have always been Fredericka as well. I'm not going to hide anymore.

I'm breaking my silence: "Nurse—I'm ready to answer all your questions, and I'm very grateful to you for listening to what I have to say."

I never forgot the image
from the bygone era of doom
the gloom-engulfed spring
that withered budding
shriveled bloom
in obscured light only conjured memory
could blend a blurred concealed face
into endless yearning

RIDE INTO THE CITY

WHENEVER I ARRIVE in a big city I feel apprehensive, as though I'm walking toward a gaping tunnel that will suck me in with the force of an enormous vacuum cleaner devouring a tiny spider.

I was about to leave the world of planned order: the even temperature, the unobtrusive lights, the neutered music, the skillfully displayed synthetic-tasting foods, highly polished floors, and, of course, the sanitary toilets. All big airports share the atmosphere of those impersonal if self-indulgent modern achievements—uniform predictability within standard procedures. It was calming and comforting.

In wintertime I feel particularly vulnerable. This January evening was no exception. There was a long line of people waiting in the raging blizzard at the exit of the airport terminal. Under different weather conditions I would not have done what I did. I would have waited patiently for my turn to get into a taxi.

But then the wind hit me. I saw the unoccupied cab moving slowly amid the heavy traffic in the middle of the street. It was odd for me to make the move I did, as there were so many other people ahead of me waiting for cabs. I disregarded the caution which usually guides my behavior.

Everything happened so fast. It was the face of the driver, which I could barely see, that had prompted my impulsive run toward his car. The car had slowed down, almost to a halt. The driver leaned back and opened the back door. I jumped in, holding my small suitcase with both hands, like a shield to protect my chest against the wind. My face felt like it was being stabbed by needles.

During those seconds in which I was running, I heard angry voices protesting my rude behavior. I tuned them out as the driver's face behind the glass panel, his expression blurred by semidarkness, distance, and snowdrift, had somehow conjured up a picture for me.

An image I had not thought about for many years flashed in front of my eyes. I was looking at the face of the driver and it was blending into an image of another—the face of a young man which I had only ever seen up close and clearly on the day he disappeared from my life.

Like so many others who were caught and taken away during the war, he never reappeared. Memory became the only place where those who vanished continued to exist. When we, the witnesses of what happened, are dead, then they who disappeared will be forgotten, gone forever.

I was sitting in a car being driven through a stormy night toward a strange city. And the face of the driver was the image of someone I had lost decades ago.

The pain of the long war spread inside me. Being a Jew, I was fair game for that most deadly team of hunters of the century. These were the rabid leaders who decided that whoever didn't fit their preconceived image of a preferred race or belief had no right to live. They chose to become masters of death.

At that time no one seemed to object, so the atrocities were carried out. War is the utmost obscenity ever conceived by man.

I had learned how to deal with losses. People who disappeared were simply not dead for me. War had deprived me of the time to mourn for those who were gone. People just vanished. Years later, some were declared dead but I, the survivor, never lost them; I felt their presence. I couldn't put those who were gone to a final rest with the old established rites, those prayers and acts which help us accept the irrevocable. All those absent from my life were merely not present. To me, they remained real; I could recall them from my memory.

During the first of the postwar years, I used to stare at the faces of people passing by on the streets, hoping to recognize someone I had known and lost. At times I would run after a person whose walk seemed familiar, or perhaps the shape of a head would provoke a memory. I hoped so much to find someone who was missing.

Later that need diminished. The past became more distant, less significant. I was moving on with my life. Images of faces and places that were no more became remote, vague. It wasn't that I had forgotten the past, but I had found a way to live and deal with the present.

The driver had adjusted the mirror and was looking at me. It was no use watching the traffic. No one could possibly be driving with any speed when the visibility was so poor. One could only see the taillights of the cars as they shone through our fast-moving windshield wipers.

I had the sensation of everything slowing down. Blinking specks of light were coming in and out of focus. Sitting in the warmth of the slow-moving car, I felt as though I was cushioned within a huge womb of densely falling snow.

What had happened to me just a short while ago? A split-second image of a face out of the depths of my memory had me running for the taxi in an impulsive attempt to recapture it. That image, that face, had sent a tremor through my whole being. I was still trembling. It was not the cold outside.

During the long flight, I had read about earthquakes. And right now I was experiencing the shifting of my inner tectonic plates. By now, boiling magma was gushing out only as I imagined and represented it in my paintings. Time was extinguishing most of the burning outbursts from the past.

This was a quivering movement reflecting back to where there had been violent inner upheavals decades ago. But the activity that could split my memory mountains surged upward once again, revealing layers buried deep within the cataclysm I had survived. Here, exposed in front of me, was an imprint from that tumultuous past, one that had solidified within the clay bed of my being. Though my past is only measured in years, this image and event seemed eons away.

The driver's face expressed the smile of a child who had gotten away with a nasty prank. He said he didn't like to wait in lines, especially with the weather turning so bad, and since I didn't have any luggage, he didn't feel he had to get out of the car. What a smile, with its broad features that looked so good from a distance, a bit large, but still beautiful at close range. I had only known the face from a distance, that face from the past. I had never seen that fateful face so close, the one of another time, another place.

The face of a person I had not thought about for many years looked at me from the rearview mirror, in a foreign city, many decades removed from the young man whose existence was real only in my memory.

Reality took on a new dimension. I was looking at several images, each one superimposed on top of the other. It had never occurred to me that emotional perception could be equipped with the dimensions that would produce such a sensation. Yet it was happening to me, right then. One of the oldest beliefs of mankind is that, if forgotten, one does not exist anymore. I had not forgotten. Right then and there, I was looking at a face that was still alive within me, preserved as I had seen it up close but once.

Like those crystal balls, suspended in time in their airtight seals, that hold freshly cut roses with dew on the petals—that is how I felt. When you look at those flowers you can practically smell them as the brain remembers the scent.

The driver must have opened the window because my face was hit by an icy breath. It jolted me. I was experiencing the winter of here and now. I've heard about people waxing poetic about gentle snow and cozy winter memories. But I cannot associate winter with a pastoral idyll. The elements raging outside and the young man's face whose half profile I was staring at brought back my recollections of war. I remembered the encircling roundup of the few who managed to escape the first mass killings in the second year of war.

Along with the cold weather came the chill of fear. At times I had to be away from my hiding place on the farm, and stayed overnight in the safe haven available to me in the city. Moving was hazardous, and so was the illusion of security in the shelters I retreated to. The hunted can never rest; indeed, they are doomed if their alertness is lost.

I was in my teens; I wanted to live. But I never got to experience being a teenager, that time span of recognition when being young means that nothing else matters. Through the years that have passed since, I've wondered what it would have been like to discover that key metamorphosis in a young person's life; how would it have felt to be in bloom?

The driver was talking hesitantly. His knowledge of the language was limited. He was a foreigner as well. I wasn't listening to what he said. And so his voice became merely background noise, like the hum of the car engine. I was so involved in my own thoughts racing back in time.

Nineteen forty-two—there was no hope for any progress in the dynamics of war. The insatiable greed of the oppressive war power machine grew constantly. It was insanity, but deprived of the grotesque element of madness that at times, even for an instant, illuminates somber events.

That was the period when I was in the darkened little room on the fifth floor. This was my hiding place in the city. Right now, in the taxi, I was recalling from memory one of the frequent curfews which dictated that I had to stay in the city after dark. That was a moment when everything seemed motionless and I wasn't sure if I or anybody else was alive. At that point it didn't even matter. I don't know if those feelings were lasting or fleeting. Time was meaningless.

Usually surges of energy would follow my inert state. This could have been the case when I stood in my city hiding place trying to find traces of life behind the black windows of the houses across the wide street. I might have been responding to the gaping hole in the middle of that street that broached the sidewalk as well. At the beginning of the invasion there had been heavy air raids and the city was partially destroyed. That bomb crater was only one of many; it made the road look like a lacerated body.

All the apartment houses as far as I could see had darkened windows. Like the burrows of tiny animals, there were empty-looking holes, but deep inside there might have been life. I believed there was—intense, suppressed, concealed life.

How many people were hiding in those darkened interiors? Though I put the thought as a question, it was comforting. Above all else, I did not want to be an isolated outcast within the world that surrounded me.

Part of my war memories are vivid, part of that time I completely blanked out. How much is left of reality when we recall past times?

What I missed most on those endless evenings was of course food. Then, to talk, to someone, anyone. It would have made a difference to have been able to express what I thought or even dared to feel. Feeling was a luxury.

Yes, talking could have eased those days that were devoid of dreams. Night only brought nightmares. Just to talk to someone my own age became my great unfulfilled need. The only positive result of that deprivation was that I have never felt lonely since.

It took years after the war for me to start a conversation with someone. I have never learned the skill of small talk. Here in the taxi, the driver was talking constantly. I had entirely missed what he was saying. He seemed to have lost some of his cheerful attitude, alternately staring out into the storm, then at my reflection in the rearview mirror, where our eyes met.

Maybe he was afraid the car would stop if he fell silent. I could feel a tension building up in the slow-moving enclosure. We were sharing an isolated privacy. Maybe I was projecting my feelings, which were becoming more intimate as I continued to experience long-buried emotions. Among them was my yearning to meet the person whose face in that faraway past I had been trying to identify, trying to fix as it moved behind the dark window across that bomb-damaged street. Here in the taxi I must have sensed the virility of the young man whose presence was starting to overwhelm me. All of a sudden I felt old, the result of being attracted to this youngster just because he looked like the man who had vanished from my life such a long time ago. A man I never really got to know.

The driver was staring at me in the mirror. What an amazing resemblance. A wave of forgotten longing was sweeping over me. It was starting to feel uncomfortable in the car. To break the silence that was closing in on me, I asked the driver to tell me about himself. Few people can resist the temptation to talk about themselves, especially if asked to. The driver responded immediately. I was only partially hearing some bits of the information he was readily giving. I didn't mean to be rude, but rather, I just wanted to be alone with my memories and the fantasies that years ago had added color to a dreary hopeless existence. Life during the war was not more than barely staying alive within hostile surroundings.

I don't recollect what my daydreams were at that time. I believe all my fantasies must have been very basic. There was no space for fancy thoughts, for escapes into dreamland. The danger lay in not wanting to return to reality. To give up reality when faced with danger meant death. So I just learned to walk the tightrope of daydreams.

The driver had stopped the car and turned his smiling face toward me. What would happen if we were stranded in the car for some time, unable to move on? His shiny dark eyes were steady as they focused on me. Was he reading my thoughts? Was I really wishing for something like that to happen? Would I then be able to rid myself of an unfulfilled longing that had started decades ago and was just covered over by time?

The absence of motion started to be unnerving. My mouth felt dry and I had difficulty breathing within the stillness. Then someone behind us started to press on the horn and the shrill noise broke the spell. The driver was again looking forward and I felt relief. No, I didn't want to be stranded with a long-abandoned daydream.

I just wanted to drift into reminiscences, to be able to recollect the darkened facade of the building from the past. I wanted to locate the window again, as I did then so long ago. Behind that window at times was the shadow of a man. I knew he was hiding. He never came near the window while there still was some daylight; neither did I. I knew he must have seen me. We would each stand for hours, a few steps back from the windowpanes, looking at each other until it became completely dark outside. At times way beyond that. Being accustomed to living in darkness, I had learned to interpret shadows. So did he.

I don't really know when it happened. What time of the year it was. Passing seasons were marked by either harsh cold winters, hard to endure, or hot humid summers bursting with life. Nature was claiming its rights, flowers were blooming, crickets were sounding their mating chirps. The in-between seasons gently burst with migrating birds that were following their eternal routes. War could not disrupt the basic laws of nature.

Whenever events forced me to move into the hiding place in the city, I could at least look forward to the anticipated reward. In the long evening that would follow my hazardous journey I was going to see my fellow fugitive across the street.

The driver had been talking for some time, looking at me in the mirror, with an apologetic smile on his face. I wasn't listening. Perhaps I nodded my head as he went on talking. I drifted away from his chatter.

I was standing on the corner of the street with the bomb crater, numbed by the scene in front of me. I had just arrived in town after hiding at the farm for some time. It was still broad daylight and I was carefully watching what was happening around me, walking slowly toward the building that held my fifth-floor hiding place. I had just turned the corner of that street that had been scarred by the cavernous bomb crater when I saw a group of Nazi soldiers. Their infamous SS insignia glared ominously as they walked toward a waiting van.

In their midst was the man who was hiding across the street. I recognized the shape of his head—the head I had seen only from a distance in semidarkness but knew well, with an intimacy gained through long observation. The young man's face was slightly turned toward me. His complexion was very pale and terror took hold of me as I stood there motionless. He was going to turn his head and look at me again. I knew that if he did, his captors would be aware of my presence. I was in danger.

The soldiers were taking him away and I knew what that meant; all I wished for was that he not turn his head. He did not. He didn't look back at me and I was grateful; I remained undetected. He knew the rules. I have never learned his name.

Streetlights were multiplying as we drove; we were entering the city. The snowstorm was receding. When we arrived at the hotel where I was staying, I thanked the driver for managing the roads so

well under difficult conditions. He refused to take the tip I offered—all he wanted was the price of the fare, he said. His face
again widened into a smile, and he thanked me for showing so
much interest when I had asked him questions and listened to his
problems. He extended his hand and was beaming when I shook it.

I got out. The car was pulling away. For an instant I saw the half
profile of the driver's head; it was an amazing resemblance. Again,
I saw a young man's head surrounded by Nazi soldiers as they were
pushing him into one of those deadly dark cars. He did not turn toward me. I remained safe. That whole event probably took seconds; it hounded me for years.

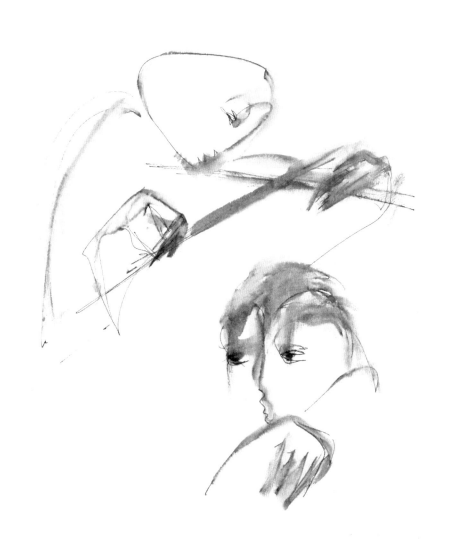

silence has not yet set in
although the music ceased
reverberating it is a theme
that has been around me
and now only an echo etched in memory
the scores are known
the instruments off key

TZIGANE

WHEN ISABELLE ORDERED HER TROUSSEAU, she had the bedsheets and spreads made out of black satin. As the news about this circulated around town, part of the community was shocked.

The younger generation of the town's Jewish families were trying to keep up with the times, yet they were also holding on to their traditions. There were many manifestations, expressions of their nostalgia for the bygone era, especially for the vanished decadent splendor of the Austro-Hungarian Empire. Bowing, kissing hands, and the like. Between the restless desire for the modern and the yearning for a romanticized past, younger people like Isabelle were groping for new self-expressive "isms."

Isabelle's home was one of the fanciest in town and the meeting place for those wanting to be part of the new wave of arts and ideas sweeping through Central Europe. Isabelle had adopted the flair of art deco, and she definitely set the pace. Her gatherings were filled with talk about art, literature, music, theater. But the real attraction on those occasions was the inevitable card game, the culmination of the social event.

Ladies of that circle would frequently travel from the Balkans to Central Europe and bring home new and enticing topics for conversation. And of course there were the results of their equally inevitable splurges in the latest styles of dress, so others in the small town could be envious and dash off to make copies of the gowns. The gentlemen of the group would go on so-called business trips. They would tour the cabarets of various European capitals, and hopefully, they would bring home only a dog, which mattered mostly because of its pedigree. The dog's lineage would have to be as long as that of the impoverished nobility who were breeding those very costly animals mostly to maintain their own deflated lifestyles. Then there were also the talented members of the Novi

Sad group who organized amateur charity performances of the current big-city shows.

Father was part of the creative segment in the group, debonair in off-white spats, homburg, bow tie, and kid gloves. How that image remains in my memory. But I also remember my father in a very different picture. The transformation occurred when he would take out his violin and play. I liked to watch and listen when he played the intense Hungarian folk songs and fierce Gypsy melodies, with their rhythms as basic as a pulse beat. As a child, I was deeply affected by both the fervor of this music and my father's deeply involved playing. The performance made me feel tense with pleasure and upset at the same time. Alone, during the long war years, I often thought how much I would have liked the chance to know Father better.

At times of respite—when the war, like a deadly illness, was in remission—I used to wonder about my parents' generation. Until the moment they and their world vanished and my home was destroyed, that generation was the arbiter of elegance and behavior for mine. My parents' generation had survived the horrifying First World War. Did they have an inkling of impending disaster before it flared up again in utterly destructive violence? They were so unprepared when the next war began.

After so many decades, I've tried to analyze and be more objective about what my own emotions were when World War II broke out in our region. The first order of the Nazi invaders was that all Jews had to register. Disobedience meant the death penalty. Every Jew had to wear a large yellow patch with the Star of David in the center. Thus identified, one was an easy target for slaughter. I remembered learning that when infectious diseases ravaged Europe in centuries past, to prevent the spread of illness every victim's household had to have a yellow sign on the door—a warning, visible from far away, to avoid this dangerous place.

We were marked in order to be kept at a distance. I remember my anger overpowering my fear. We were regarded by the Nazis as unclean, contaminated, dangerous to be near. These arrogant representatives of power first debased, then killed everyone who had registered. I felt enraged at being persecuted, hunted like a rabid animal, when I was a decent, rational, thinking teenager who had done no harm to anyone.

There was a hill in the middle of town where big country fairs and other festivities were usually held. This was the place chosen by the Nazi command to be the site where the Jews had to register. Silent rows of Jewish families stood in meticulous alphabetical order. Everyone, even small children, wore the yellow mark.

Father's anger must have had an intensity similar to mine. My family wordlessly left the line that was slowly moving toward doom. We said good-bye to each other. Alone, each one took his chance. We were the ones who survived.

Following the end of war, the unimaginable, mechanically efficient mass murder became history. The Nazi brutality is duly recorded in the dry statistics of the event called World War II. In their meticulous manner, the Nazi murderers prepared and stored the neatly arranged files documenting their efficient destruction. They must have been proud of preserving the information as a hallmark of their national heritage, a collection of memorabilia for posterity.

It was many years later that I met Isabelle again. She remembered me vaguely, as one of the kids from the prewar era, she said. She invited me to her home, and I gratefully accepted. There were not many people around who would ask me to visit them.

Isabelle had aged way beyond her years. That was true for all survivors. By now she had found a new group of card players, but the gatherings lacked the flair of the prewar assembly. I wondered whether theirs was a brave attempt to reconstruct a vanished era or whether it was cowardice about venturing into a changed reality.

I participated in some of these strangely ghostlike and ageless get-togethers. Middle age was unkind to these veterans of dying and of living beyond death. Isabelle still had some of the mannerisms I remembered and admired as a child. One of them was her complete lack of interest in practical daily chores. Somebody always took over, or the work just wasn't done.

In spite of the devastating experiences in Isabelle's life, her vague approach to just about everything had not changed. This could have been the reason she had managed to survive one of the most notorious death camps in the Nazis' regime. I didn't ask her about that time. I wasn't ready to talk about myself, either.

One day, during a chance encounter with Isabelle, she started talking in her unpredictable way: "You probably know I played the cello as a young girl. It was easier than the violin, and I liked the way I could embrace the instrument. My whole body was involved. I never became even a fair musician. But playing did save my life.

"It must have been one of those murderous minds that was behind the perverse idea to form an orchestra in the death camp," Isabelle continued. "There were former members of some European symphonies. I believe the Nazi commander of the camp put me into the orchestra as the ultimate insult to those musicians. I never played in tune.

"Most of us were barely alive, the same as those walking toward the ever belching chimneys. We were holding on to our instruments, our only link to another day, trying not to show any deficiency. Weakness meant death; I tried to play as correctly as I possibly could—my life depended on it."

I had a vision of emaciated faces, shaven skulls, musical instruments protruding out of colorless rags, bony fingers playing music while endless lines of people were being marched into the gas chambers.

Isabelle's muted voice continued: "At some time Leo became concertmaster. He was such a brilliant musician. What a wasted career."

Leo, my father—how I used to watch him, leaning his head on the smooth wood with a loving touch, gently putting his hand around the fingerboard just below the pegs, lifting the bow.

Isabelle looked like a shriveled leaf. A cloud of sadness descended upon me. She continued in a whisper: "Leo was an artist. He held us together with the strength of his big musical repertoire and his daring humor. Sometimes he would sneak in some Offenbach themes into the Viennese waltzes we were playing.

The Germans never realized that. We of course were terrified and delighted.

"I don't know how long we continued to play, for weeks, months, always accompanying those death marchers. The orchestra kept diminishing in size. We all knew those who didn't show up in the morning would never be seen again."

Isabelle looked completely gray. I didn't think a live person's complexion could develop that shade. I saw her as she must have looked in the camp, embracing the cello. If she played, she existed. Ravaged by starvation, playing music in the ultimate degradation of humanity.

I could see the endless lines of human shadows moving slowly toward buildings with smoking chimneys. For me this was going to be a lifelong source of horror-filled dreams, not to mention my waking hours. For Isabelle, this had been reality.

Isabelle's barely audible voice became gray as well: "When Leo fell ill, we were all very frightened. Who was going to lead the orchestra if he didn't show up in the morning? He was weakening, and could barely hold the violin."

There was a long pause. I wasn't sure if she was going to continue. My father had never returned. By now the pain was only in the brain, like the sensation long after an amputation—the missing part is always present in the nerve center of an amputee.

Isabelle was talking again. I wasn't sure if I had missed something but didn't dare to interrupt.

"One day there was a group marching toward the chimneys; yet in spite of their shaven heads and rags, they looked different. They walked erect, with an aura of pride. Leo knew who they were, as he had always liked them. 'They are Gypsies,' he said sadly. 'They are proud to have been put into the same category as we Jews.'"

Isabelle's voice seemed to have gained strength when she continued: "Leo took his violin and started to play Ravel's 'Tzigane.'" His playing was a triumphal ode for the doomed Gypsies. "When he finished, he put down his violin and walked off. I never saw him again."

I felt an upsurge of gratitude toward Isabelle. It had been difficult for her to share that memory.

I was fifteen when my family dispersed, each on his own, to try and survive. We had all agreed to that decision. Actively taking that chance, together and yet to be separated, was all that was left of our self-respect.

Hearing Isabelle's reminiscences, I felt pain. I also felt pride. At least I knew that Father had made the choice to die with dignity. It was, until the end, his way to live.

comforting language gone
and a place with childhood memories to recount home
vile power scourge
swept away in blind urge
like a tidal wave crushed uprooted laid waste
with no nourishing ingredient of water
restoring nature
an opaque dangerous tide
spread poisoned ground
where only seeds of hate could germinate
we are soaring in space
enveloped by a blue sky's protective shield
which guards us not to get lost in a dark universe
that keeps ultimate laws from being revealed
if our ruthless limitless nature
at times concealed
breaks loose
nothing can save us from being drawn
into our own black hole
of voracious violence
wanton destruction

SULTANA

W HEN THE DOOR OPENED I KNEW I HAD FOUND the right house. I had been told which road to take after leaving the city of Belgrade, including the distance and approximate stretches of woods surrounding the area. Where to turn in order to get to the dirt road leading to the house, and finally, a description of the family that was going to give me shelter. I knew it was vital for me to locate the place before dark; there was a curfew.

Walking fast, in spite of the heavy backpack I carried, I couldn't help looking at the people all around, painstakingly carrying their bundled-up belongings. Dazed silent people dragging loaded pushcarts, frightened small children sitting on top of the chaotic piles. After the relentless bombing, life was draining out of the city. The wide road seemed to narrow as the side streets became filled with more people moving south. They were going toward the rolling hills which promised respite from the acrid stench of burning buildings and the people who were caught in them.

I was afraid of being slowed down, caught within the growing mob. I had to get out of the city fast and to find the farmhouse I was looking for. After hours of vigorous walking I was still within the city. Open country appeared far away, and my load seemed heavier all the time. I accurately remembered the drawing I had made of the scattered small forests, the winding dirt road, and the distance from the woods to the house. My goal was to reach the outskirts of the city and open fields before dark.

I was told not to ask any questions. There was no space for a mistake, for knocking on a wrong door. I had been given the names of the two women, but not the family name of the man in the house. In case I was caught and questioned by the German patrols who were moving between the exhausted refugees, I did not have an address or the name of the family to implicate them; it was safer that way.

After I gathered my courage and knocked, I was relieved when the old woman who answered the front door matched the description I had been given. Extremely exhausted from my long journey and heavy load, I was close to tears, but that was no place to cry. The owners of the tiny farm had agreed to give me shelter, to hide me from the Nazi occupiers. The peasants wanted a worker, not a tearful kid who has just parted from her family and ventured into an alien existence. They knew I came from a privileged background, and the last thing I was going to allow myself was to acknowledge and show my weakness.

Many hours ago, I had said good-bye to my sister, mother, and father. My father was going to try and cross two borders to the north of Belgrade: first into Croatia, granted its freedom for collaborating with the Nazis, then farther north to where my grandmother lived. That territory, part of the former Austro-Hungary, was lost in the armistice of 1918, and was being returned to Hungarian rule after the Nazis occupied Serbia proper in April 1941. On the other hand, Yugoslavia, which had been formed by carving up other countries, did not exist anymore. All that just within one generation. History could be extremely amusing if not for the human suffering involved.

Father was planning a dangerous escape, but he sounded confident. All of us were covering our fears by showing self-reliance. Father was the first to leave. Then I said good-bye to my mother and sister. They planned to move into a small apartment. I was sure I'd be with them someday.

When I passed over the threshold of the farmhouse, south of Belgrade, I entered a new existence. The old woman standing in the door frame was shorter than I. She seemed to resent that, perhaps expecting a small, frail fifteen-year-old. She lifted her dark expressionless eyes for a short while, looking at me with a penetrating stare. Her face was like dry parchment, wrinkled, revealing neither emotion nor age. I was brought up to greet people with a smile, but this was very difficult for me at that moment, despite my relief that the door had not been slammed in my face. I felt frightened, hungry, sad, and at the end of my strength. For hours I had been carrying a heavy load of carefully packed crystal glasses, fine silver utensils, and some damask linen. As part of the terms of my stay, I was supposed to deliver all of this to the farmers. In addition, a sum of money had been previously sent through the person who found the shelter for me.

The first load was part of my sister's and my trousseaux; I was to bring the rest of it to the farm within the next few days. It was urgent that I accomplish this shuttling back and forth to the city while the occupation was just beginning. This first stage was complete chaos, with so many aimless, moving people on the roads— people trying to survive an onslaught that was the harbinger of great disasters.

The occupying forces were in a hurry to establish their order. At a later time it would be more dangerous for me to move without my identification papers; I knew speed was necessary.

I was now following the old woman, who had not spoken or looked at me again. She was wearing the traditional sort of garment for a widow, consisting of a tight kerchief around her head and a shapeless long dress, all in black. She told me her name was Sultana, and when I inquired about the origin of that non-Serbian-sounding name, I was told not to ask questions.

The young woman who opened the inner door was rather good-looking. She was the lady of the house. I wouldn't meet her husband for another couple of days. Both women revered him, but only the wife talked to him, whereas the mother-in-law was silent, submissive. This was all part of a different culture, one I had to get used to. That first evening I was so utterly exhausted, I hardly paid attention when the young woman, named Lepa, which meant "beautiful," showed me the part of the house that was to be my dwelling. During the coming days I found out more about my new reality.

My room was adjacent to, but not connected to, the house. The dogs were to sleep inside with me in bad weather, Lepa said. With a large wooden bench to sleep on, it was a room for a farm laborer. The mattress was filled with straw that still had the lingering scent of freshness; I liked that. There was an outhouse at some distance and a water pump a couple of yards away. This water was only to be used for washing and for the animals. For drinking water, Lepa gave me two large tin canisters with tight lids. I was to go in the morning as early as possible to fetch drinking water. When I asked about the location of the source, Lepa said I would see where everyone went with their buckets and I was just to follow. With that she left me in my room and I fell asleep on the bed with my clothes on. I had started a new path in my life.

Carrying water was a daily routine. The cans were heavy and the way partially uphill. After bringing water that first day, I had to hurry into the city and be back before evening. It took a couple of days of my running against time to bring what I was supposed to back to the farm.

It grew more and more hazardous to leave my hiding place. I might be observed walking toward the main road day after day, and someone could report me. The purpose of my last two walks to the city was to bring the books I wanted to have with me. Always valued in my own home, books became necessary to me now, so I took volumes of our encyclopedia out of the oak bookcase in my former home, and brought them to the farm. The two women were puzzled that I made these long journeys just to carry heavy books. I wanted these books for a couple of reasons. My whole life was going to be changed for the unknown duration of the war. I did not exist legally, and was thus deprived of continuing my education. It felt good to have the books close by, even though time for reading became very limited. There was no electricity, and daylight hours for reading were scarce.

Decades later I realized those volumes represented my identity, symbols from my life as it was before the war.

Lepa, who was only partially literate, found the books fascinating, until she realized they represented a world she was not familiar with, in a language she did not know, either. My books probably created a gap in our future communications. Lepa laughed at my wanting to keep the books in a crate, where the mice couldn't nibble on them. She must have realized how far my world was from hers. She made it clear to me that I was on a farm now, and had better let go of my fancy past.

It was a shock for me to adjust to the painfully difficult, demeaning, and dreary beginning of my new life. What probably ameliorated the situation was my feeling of gratitude to these people for taking such a great risk for me. Though at times my chores seemed to be at the very edge of my physical ability, I never complained. Of course I felt indebted to the family that provided me with shelter. I knew their monetary compensation was no exchange for what they offered me. I promised them that if searched for, I'd run, even be shot, but I would not implicate them.

A difficulty I had not anticipated at the beginning of my farm life was just talking to Lepa and her mother. After my arrival, when I greeted Sultana with a good morning, she called me Baksoos, which meant "bad luck." This was a Turkish word, an idiom used in Serbia. I didn't know the reason for that unpleasant response, but it never varied over the years. At some point I started to believe that maybe it was Sultana's superstitious way of protecting the whole household, including me, against the evil eye.

I tried to understand Sultana's Macedonian dialect, which sounded similar to the Serbian language, but with additional Turkish and Greek words. At times both women were talkative, recounting to me fragments out of their past. But it was always the same story, like looking at a faded photograph one cannot put away.

For me their memories were like windows, giving me a glimpse of a world I did not know and a time before I was born.

One event they talked about many times seemed to represent Sultana's whole life story. It centered around the assassination of her husband by political rivals. He had been an elected representative in their rural region. One day a group of men gunned him down, and Sultana had to flee with her two little boys and Lepa, who was a baby, leaving behind everything they had in the house. She just took her children and ran. Considering this was a time of peace in the country, such violence was startlingly sinister. These events surprised me and made me feel ignorant of life. It occurred to me now that there must have been political struggles taking place in remote areas that never made the daily news. Sultana's story continued with the local authority helping her escape hidden in a cart loaded with hay. A short story that devastated a whole family, with lifelong effects for the two women.

Sultana was receiving a pension from the Yugoslav government for her husband's work and death, and was given the opportunity to stay in the city of Belgrade for the safety and education of her children. She seemed to be proud of the fact that her husband was so important in the political life of the region that his opponents had no way to defeat him. They had to kill him.

As a young woman it was probably very hard for Sultana to live far from her home turf and family. I must have said this when I heard the story for the first time, but Sultana told me to shut up. She never talked about her family or where they lived; it seemed odd, but of course I did not ask again.

At first I was amused by the obscene language the mother and daughter used in conversation. When urged to talk that way my-self, I refused, claiming I'd never be authentic. It seemed a good way not to offend them. I was just not used to cursing. The man in the house must have been consulted in the matter; he told me that the best way not to sound peculiar around people would be not to talk at all. Thus my four years of silence had begun.

He also advised me not to look anyone in the eye. I was sup-posed to act feebleminded so that I wouldn't be an object of suspi-cion. Thus was I isolated from what had become my surroundings. Since I wouldn't adopt the crude language flowing between mother and daughter, Lepa said that if I couldn't stop using my educated way of speaking, I had better not talk to the two of them either. She might have meant it as a rebuke, but I received it as a favor, provid-ing me with privacy. Silence became a safe place for me to with-draw into from the obscenities and crude behavior.

My duties also included feeding and taking care of the animals, which was the work I liked. Especially the newly hatched chickens. Cleaning off the parasites that clung to their tiny heads was like playing with fluffy little toys, but it was also essential to their sur-vival. If they were not removed, these parasites would eventually kill the chicks. The chickens considered me a mother hen and used to follow me.

I also groomed the dogs, and this provided me with the physical warmth I lacked. I grew fond of the animals, and even stopped feeling disgusted by the pigs I regularly washed and brushed and whose sty I cleaned. The pigs became attached to me, but somehow I never developed a relationship with the hogs. I started cleaning the pigs for my own comfort because of the odor, but I soon realized that the pigs loved to be clean. They wallowed in dirt in order to protect their sensitive skin from blood-sucking parasites.

The difficult part of my work was sawing and chopping logs. The first part was physically demanding. Chopping with the large hatchet was frightening. I knew if I injured my hands in the process, there was no way for me to get medical attention.

Washing large piles of laundry involved a series of complex heavy chores. Preparing the firewood in order to heat the water in the big cauldron, lifting the washed sheets and hanging them, was especially difficult in winter, when my hands became frozen and swollen. There were also occasional trips to the mill to grind wheat. The sacks equaled my own body weight, which made them tedious to lift, and then I would climb the ladder to pour the contents into the funnel to be ground. I developed strong muscles from all of this.

During the second year of the war, Lepa was given a concession from the local Serbian authority to sell tobacco and cigarettes. She leased a tiny shop in one of the bombed-out parts of Belgrade. The shop was on a crossroad with easy access in and out of the city. There was a very good reason for that location, as I came to find out.

Lepa had to sell the merchandise to everyone who had a ration card with a special provision for tobacco. That was the law. Having the permit to buy and sell gave Lepa the opportunity to get some of the rationed commodity for herself, and she would barter the cigarettes on the black market. This of course was illegal, and I was asked to take part in the more dangerous phase of the project. I knew I could be caught only once.

Needless to say, I was afraid, but being a teenager, I also had a sense of invincibility. This lent the flavor of adventure to my otherwise difficult and dull existence. Besides that, I had agreed to do whatever the farmers asked. Lepa said that she had to have extra income and benefits, and tobacco created that opportunity. She would not have asked me to participate otherwise, she said, and I believed her.

I began to plan how I would smuggle the packages of cigarettes out of the shop. It had to be done fast while a sale was in progress. I sewed deep pockets into the shapeless garment I wore, a kind of overshirt. I figured out how to fill those inside pockets with cigarettes and take the highly valued merchandise out of the shop, stashed away on my body. My main concern was the people standing in line waiting to buy the precious commodity. I knew they would be suspicious of me walking out of the shop while there was still tobacco on the shelves.

What I didn't anticipate, and which gave me a terrible jolt when I entered Lepa's shop on her first day in business, was the presence of a German soldier, supervising the proceedings with his rifle drawn.

Years later, after the war had ended, I tried to understand and clarify for myself what had made me react the way I did then— when I realized the danger standing in the corner, the German soldier with his gun facing the window through which Lepa was selling her tobacco. And there was only one door, close to where the soldier stood. I was in a trap.

I completely disregarded the presence of that soldier and started to hand the packages from the shelves to Lepa at the counter. It was what we had agreed upon when we planned the pilfering of her merchandise. We had rehearsed what I was supposed to do, which was to pile up the packages on my chest and hold them to my chin, then slip a couple of them into my inner pockets on the way from the shelves to the window, where the sale took place. Lepa liked the idea. And that was exactly what I did.

The soldier with the gun was watching, but I did what I was supposed to do anyway. The instant I had my back to him, I slipped several packages through the opening around my neck, and into the pockets on the inside of my shirt. This was how Lepa and I planned the whole project, and it worked.

After my pockets were filled, I told Lepa I had to leave. I had not even looked at the soldier; I just opened the door and started to walk. In her loud harsh voice, Lepa was explaining to people in front of the window that I was a sick girl who had to relieve myself frequently.

Lepa had instructed me where to take the cigarettes I had smuggled out. When she first took the shop, I went with her to help put the shelves back into place, to clean the floor and windows, and to make the place look more like it had before it had become as rundown as its surroundings. Just a couple of yards away used to be a residential complex, now bombed out. A large mountain of rubble from exploded houses nobody would or could repair was a reminder of the vicious destruction at the beginning of the war. The ruins were an area everyone avoided, as one never knew what part of the demolished houses would collapse under one's feet.

I thought this was the best route I could take with my load of contraband, to be sure that no one would follow me and grab what was hidden on my person. Because I weighed little, I was confident about walking over, or around, large gaping holes in the ruins. Although there were scores of rats in these bombed-out dwellings, I was only slightly afraid of them. I was more afraid of the harm people could do to me.

Walking for the first time on that hazardous ground, with my pockets filled with cigarettes, I felt relief when my feet finally hit the rubble of hanging pieces of concrete and I could look into the depths of collapsed apartments. I had just made my way out of a dangerous situation. There was the soldier, keeping order in case of disturbances. And there were the hundreds of people standing in line, hungry and angry. I feared that mob outside the shop, watching me walking out the door. I was sure they knew I had taken some of the precious tobacco and had thus deprived them of it.

I did not dare turn my head and look back. No one was following me. It took me a long time that first day to walk over the shafts and broken concrete blocks hanging over the gaping holes of sunken buildings in that bombed-out area. If I slipped and fell, I knew there was absolutely no one to try and find me, except for the rats. I paid a great deal of attention to every step I took. The further I advanced over the ruins, the more I feared losing my balance and falling. I did not dare tremble, as the ground itself was shaky. I had to make my way slowly to a higher point in order to get a better view of my direction, where I would come out on the opposite side of the destroyed area.

I was searching for a butcher Lepa knew; the plan was that he would give me money and meat for the cigarettes. I was to meet him in a wooden shack he had in a row of abandoned storage facilities on the other side of that bombed-out housing project. I had to find his hideout, where he practiced his trade in secret; that was what I was told.

I knew the touch of fear, and how it could take over my whole body, sinking its claws into the region of my belly and making me tremble. Then the grip would crawl up until it got hold of my throat, choking me until my mouth would be completely dry. If I was not careful enough to find the place on this first attempt, I would have to go back to the farm without having accomplished what was expected of me. I didn't want to fail after getting this far on my perilous mission.

I must have learned it from the dogs: to lift my head and sniff the air for odors different from those that were part of the surroundings. Like those of the dumps, with their stench of decaying bodies buried in the ruins and never retrieved after the bombing, a stench that had dissipated over the two years. Now there was just dust and the stale smell of broken walls and plaster. There was also a distinct odor that revealed the presence of generations of rodents that had made their burrows in the cavernous ruins.

After a while I could smell it. Slaughter had a distinct odor, and it became more prominent if I moved in a particular direction. I knew I had better remember how to orient myself, as the butcher was going to be my destination the next time I could sneak out with more tobacco. The smell of the butcher shop came from where the ruins led, into what looked like an abandoned backyard. In the past it probably housed small workshops and storage shacks. Now it seemed desolate except for the smell, and when I could slow my breath that was echoing in my ears, I could hear the chopping sound of a hatchet. I had found the butcher.

Getting away from the rubble, I found myself on a narrow path. In front of one of the shacks was a woman sitting on a chair looking at me. She was extremely fat. Her body was flowing over the rather large chair and her presence dominated the narrow walkway. I could not guess her age because her face was not only round but devoid of wrinkles. She was dressed in what might have been well made years ago, but by now was shabby and too small. Her hair was dyed black, showing traces of neglected coloring, and she wore heavy makeup. She looked unreal and grotesque in those surroundings. Yet I was relieved to see someone who could not catch me if I had to run.

Then a man came out of the dark shack. He was short and thin and very pale, with sunken eyes. He looked ill, wearing a blood-smeared apron. Almost bald, unkempt, with bloody hands holding a large knife. It was the butcher I was looking for. He told me to give his wife the cigarettes. She opened a package and handed him one, which he immediately lit, drawing heavily on it. There was almost a smile lighting up his face. After a couple of puffs, he brought out of the dark, ill-smelling room a package wrapped in newspaper. The paper seemed damp, and the woman gave me more newspapers. She was the one running the business. With the additional paper, I had to make a neat bundle that would not reveal its contents until I reached the farm. I was transporting what was, if I were stopped, lethal for me to be carrying. The woman also gave me a bundle of banknotes, which I put into my now empty inner pocket.

Having taken the train, Lepa arrived some time after I had reached the farm. Since I was fast on my feet, I had walked all the way, through the shortcuts I had discovered; it was safer. Confronted by a roadblock, I could have tossed the package. In the train I would have been trapped and, moreover, the smell of meat might have been noticed as well. I didn't have the money for the train fare, anyway.

On my return, Sultana wanted to know what had taken place. She was eager to listen to my story. She was almost amused. When I described the butcher and his wife, especially how the woman looked, she even smiled at my comments.

Though tobacco deliveries to the shop were infrequent, my dreaded ordeal was repeated every couple of weeks. Nonetheless, there was some advantage in getting away from the day-in, day-out dreariness of the farm. "Tobacco Days" were days of danger. The reaction would hit me when I was back in my room and could close the door on the events of the day. I couldn't stop myself from shivering, or from having the nightmares that followed.

Lepa compensated me for my participation with some money and tobacco. I saved some of it to bring as a gift when I went into town to see my mother and sister, and I myself started to smoke.

On sale days I tried not to follow a routine, not to show a pattern to anyone who might have been watching my movements. Sometimes I stayed in the shop till the final sale, a sitting duck, my pockets filled with stolen merchandise. I would leave just before Lepa closed the shop. Moving very quickly toward the ruins with my contraband load, I soon learned to fear that assemblage of rotting debris which in the rain became treacherous, slippery passages. It was hard to keep my balance without holding on to what at times were rusty iron rods hanging from the broken concrete. I feared that if I grabbed the dangling rods, they might bring down random chunks from the broken buildings.

I started to fear the butcher. Maybe the whole ordeal of my smuggling operation with its risk of being caught was getting to me. The distasteful smell of the meat, which, despite my hunger, I never wanted to eat, anyway, was nauseating. My involvement in the scheme became a heavy burden for me. I was also disgusted by the butcher's wife, with that greedy look on her quivering face. There was the patience of a large spider in her motionless bulk, sitting in front of the vile-smelling place, grabbing what I brought. She would dole out to the man only a small portion of what he craved, and he would look at her with hatred. She observed him with glee and contempt. I dreaded witnessing their spiteful relationship.

One day I arrived for the barter in the morning, instead of my customary afternoon time. I had already taken the cigarettes for the butcher, and was approaching his shack from another direction, not over the ruins as usual. The woman was absent. The butcher must have observed my arrival, because he was on the street with the package in hand; the door to the shack was shut and secured with a rusty hanging padlock. He told me that his wife had left town. I hadn't asked where she was. There was a horrendous stench emanating from behind the closed door. He then gave me an additional small package, for me, he said, because I was taking such a risk in bringing him the cigarettes. I was surprised and moved by his words. No one else ever mentioned my efforts. He told me he was going to be away for some time.

I felt relieved not to have to return to that horrible-smelling place. When I reported to Lepa what had happened, Sultana, always in the background, chuckled. "So he got rid of her, finally killed her, after all the years of torture. He'll go away and will not be back."

She and Lepa seemed pleased. I didn't ask them, but they apparently knew the couple from before the war. All I wanted was to forget the smell of death that enveloped the ruins of the demolished houses, the butcher, and his meat supplies.

Then tobacco distribution became less restricted. The German army stopped sending soldiers to supervise sales. Soldiers were going to the eastern front. Lepa made new connections with her marketing talent and promoted to supervisor some of the men who regularly stood in line to buy cigarettes. Keeping order in the line of buyers earned them extra tobacco. Shortly afterward, Lepa closed the store. Tobacco was not such a scarce commodity anymore. It was the third year of war. I must have been in a state of dulled existence, doing my work on the farm automatically, devoid of any significance in life.

Not much has remained in my memory from that bleak, meaningless period. My body was rebelling against basic food deprivation. I started to develop swellings, boils that burst into wounds. My gums were bleeding, and when my hair started to fall out, I stopped looking in the mirror.

This was also the time when I lost my fear of being discovered. Spring of the fourth year of the war started tumultuously. There were changes in the dynamic of the war. I was invited more frequently to listen to the forbidden news broadcasts on the radio in the farmhouse. We knew about German vehicles cruising in and around the city, each one equipped with a device that could detect the strictly prohibited BBC radio broadcasts. It was the death penalty for anyone caught listening; yet the desire to be informed outweighed the threat. My farmer acquired a good radio, and I would translate the news from a couple of languages and give them the reports from the fronts and the resistance.

There was some hope that the war was going to end, but there were also the horrendous revelations of atrocities carried out by the Nazis, forming a reality difficult to come to terms with. Battles were coming closer to Belgrade. It was risky to venture into the city, so my contact with mother and sister was almost nonexistent at that time. As days went by, with the city submerged in heavy door-to-door fighting, I knew I had to go and see what was happening. During the war years I had developed an uneasy feeling whenever danger was closing in. My sister was involved with some partisan activities, and I was afraid Mother might be alone.

I had noticed throughout the war years how Mother was getting more and more dependent on someone being near her; she seemed at a loss if left alone. I decided to visit the partially freed city while the fighting was still going on. Lepa was worried when I said I had to see what was happening to my mother and sister. For the first time, she revealed that she was afraid I might get hurt. She did care for me. Her husband didn't say anything. Sultana took me to the front door, to let me out as she had let me in almost four years ago. There was an expression on her otherwise stern face that surprised me; it was friendly. She looked at me with her dark eyes and said: "I will take care of your books until you come to get them."

"you are a friend of mine a clown like I
open your door and show me in
as moonlight glows outside"
tender words of a nursery rhyme
"my candle has died
there is a word I wish to write"
simple quest in the lullaby tune
to put a child to rest
we all have cradle songs
threads woven into cloth
the fabric we wrap around
or drag behind us on the ground
but hold on to fast
then doors get slammed
no melody just harsh sounds that last
rebound when sunlight dims
and grim clouds close in
I inert on a way
with side roads of bolted gates
view through slivers reveal
real shelter behind locks
devoid of key and lack of light
I cannot find the word to write

THE FRIEND

L ONG BEFORE I MET HIM, I had heard a lot about Radomir from Mrs. Mileva. There was always a tone of reverence in her voice when she spoke about him. He was a writer.

It was during the battles around and in the city of Belgrade that I first met Mrs. Mileva. She was middle-aged, maybe a bit younger than my mother. My encounter with her took place when I came to the city in search of my mother and sister. Not finding them where they used to live, I walked out of the house with a feeling of utter emptiness.

They should have been in the apartment where I had seen them last. The door was unlocked, the apartment devoid of any life. Only my footsteps echoed in the rooms. I was frightened as I had not been for a long time. There was that burning sensation of bitterness trickling down my throat, the dried-up tears I was so familiar with. I knew my mother and sister were gone, far from the apartment. They were dead.

I never saw my sister again. Mother did return, but had lost the charming, playful attitude toward life that had made her such a strong influence on people around her. She never regained her joie de vivre, the way it used to be. That beautiful part of her was gone forever. Dead as the loved ones she had lost—her husband and daughter.

The woman calling my name from across the street was a stranger to me, but she obviously knew who I was. Her hair was dark, with some gray, and pulled back from her face in a tight bun. My grandmother had had that same hairdo. It was the only way one could manage such abundant curly hair.

The woman's eyes were dark and velvety and she looked at me with a kind, sad smile. I knew she was Jewish. I recognized the face I had never seen before. Mother had talked to me about Mrs. Mileva, who lived across the street. Neither of us ever learned her family name. Mother had met her when they were both standing in line for food. Of course, their meeting showed utter disregard of caution. Since she was in the precarious position of being in hiding, Mother was not supposed to engage in any conversation with a stranger, but she trusted people because she herself was incapable of deception.

Mother told me that Mrs. Mileva had been married for many years to a Greek Orthodox man from Cerna Gora (Montenegro), that mountainous region in the southeast. Mrs. Mileva herself was a Sephardic Jew. Her family had lived on the Balkan Peninsula for many generations.

Something I had been taught as a child, even before the war, was never to probe into what people didn't talk about. It was considered very bad manners to ask personal questions. So all I ever knew about Mrs. Mileva and her husband and family was that little bit of background.

Leaving the desolate apartment where I had desperately hoped to find my mother and sister, I was in terror. I didn't know where to go, but had to move on. It was impossible to stay and face the emptiness of the rooms, especially with their walls threatening to close in on me. One of my nightmares after the first bombardment at the beginning of the war was about suffocating, about being buried alive. This time it wasn't a horrifying dream; this time it seemed real. I felt as though I were buried alive. I had to get out fast.

At a loss, aimless, I stood in front of the building. There was that woman; I felt sure it was Mrs. Mileva calling me. Nobody else would have known my name. I held the dog, my closest link to life, tightly across my chest, like a shield, and crossed the street. There was shooting nearby.

I had heard the whistling bullets on my long trek into the city and had decided to walk only in the middle of the main wide streets. That way I was highly visible, especially in the isolated pockets of fighting in the city. Some buildings harbored lonely snipers. No one could mistakenly believe I was part of any fighting group. I was a short skinny girl, dressed in rags, carrying a dog in my arms. It felt good to have his head on my shoulder. If someone took aim at me, it would be less lonely to die this way.

Even years later, when I tried to analyze my behavior of that time, I could not come up with an explanation for why I had made such a nonrational decision to go into a city that was still a war zone. I could have stayed on the farm a little longer. It must have simply been an urge to move away from where I was. The farmers didn't try to convince me to stay. The young woman said she was going to miss me because I was a good worker. The man was morose, silent as always. Only the farmer's mother seemed relieved that I was going away. During the four years of my hiding she used to call me Baksoos, which meant bad luck, a Turkish word assimilated into the Serbian language. For four years that was her greeting for me every morning. She must have been superstitious.

So there was Mrs. Mileva calling, opening her door to me. I only had to cross a street with bullets whistling by. I needed her warm smile badly, and maybe she knew where my family was. She did not, however, have any information for me.

There were other people in Mileva's apartment. I must have looked odd, as they greeted me with curious glances. The room was crowded. They were strangers to me. Though it was kind of her to invite me, Mrs. Mileva made me feel uncomfortable. I was not used to kindness anymore.

I sat on the floor in a corner. It was not difficult for me to be silent. I hadn't really talked to people for four years. On the farm there had been only the most basic verbal exchanges, stating what had to be done, but no conversation.

On my rare, short visits with my mother and sister I didn't talk much either. They would provide me with some information about themselves, yet never inquired about my own life. They couldn't have improved my existence anyway. My ability and need to talk must have diminished greatly during those years.

In Mileva's living room I was sitting in the midst of people who I believed felt friendly toward me; yet for many hours, no one asked me anything. They were talking; I was not listening. Like a mummy, entirely dried up, devoid of any internal organs, I felt myself to be an empty shell. Maybe that was how all those people perceived me.

My dog was asleep, his head on my feet. At the instant when his body stiffened and he buried his head under my arm, I knew he had heard an alarming noise before anyone else could; he was warning me of imminent danger.

I braced myself when the bomb hit. It was close and the house was shaking from the air pressure. The detonation was deafening and even though the windowpanes were taped, fragments of glass flew all over the place. Everyone in the room was shouting, frightened. Neither I nor the dog had moved from the corner of the room where we had been sitting on the floor for hours. There was nothing to do. We were all alive. The shell had exploded very close by, but not on us. Perhaps someone else was hit. People were talking all at the same time, showing their agitation. All of a sudden, I noticed everyone in the room looking at me. Then someone said that I needed to be taken care of because I was in severe shock. The young woman who made that statement said that as a practicing nurse, she had seen this before. I had not reacted to the explosion as they had. In her opinion, this was a sign that I was not aware of reality.

Maybe she was right—but she didn't know that I might have been in shock for the last four years; my reality had been so different from theirs. To me, the explosion was just a big noise. I knew it was so much simpler to let everyone accept me as being disconnected from what was going on. Years of living on a different plane than the one I grew up on had left me with what could be considered unusual reactions, behavior that was at odds with what was considered normal and predictable under given circumstances. I realized that.

I spent that night curled up beside my dog on the floor, in the same corner where I had sat the previous day in Mileva's apartment. I might have stayed there a couple of days.

I don't remember how long it was before Mother came back. She had accompanied my sister and her friend to the partisan headquarters, where they had joined the fighters. My sister's friend was a photographer and courier. Mother said that my sister and her friend promised that they would contact her as soon as the fighting was over. I knew I would never see my sister again, but Mother was convinced otherwise.

Mrs. Mileva became a close friend of my mother's. I was extremely pleased about that. Mother's whole life had changed dramatically, not only because of her experience in hiding, but because of what happened to her family. We knew about the rounding up and deportation of the remaining Jews in Hungary. Father and Grandmother were killed at Auschwitz. Mother had acknowledged that, but long after the war was over, she still had not given up hope of my sister returning. For decades that hope did, in a way, keep her alive.

My postwar years were like exhausting races to accomplish and balance the dynamics of everyday necessities. Having missed four years of my life, I now had to earn a living, to finish my interrupted education, and take care of my mother. I saw Mrs. Mileva infrequently. But when we did meet, she almost always talked about Radomir, her close friend. The writer, she would state with pride, who was accumulating material for the book he was working on. During one of my encounters with Mrs. Mileva, she said that her friend Radomir wanted to meet me because she had told him I was studying at the Academy of Art. Needless to say, I was pleased about being introduced to a writer who showed interest in my work and so I made sure to be at her house when he came to visit.

I had always relied on my first impression of people, an awareness that had intensified during my years in hiding. Radomir was a kind and gentle human being. To me, the visual person, he looked like someone surrounded by a bubble with inner light. That was the way I would have painted him then. Many years later he does appear in some of my paintings, just like that.

He must have been way past fifty when I met him. Almost completely bald, with a deeply wrinkled face, missing teeth, and large dark soft eyes like Mrs. Mileva's. Radomir spoke hesitantly, with some difficulty. That meant he must have been in solitary confinement during the war. He looked shabby, but that was the way we all were.

Radomir was working on a project, gathering material to help him work through and bring conclusion to his ideas, he explained to me. He was collecting pictures to illustrate diverse human emotions and had all that material in files. The pictures helped him interpret ideas for his writing. I understood that. I liked the man. There was a sincerity in whatever he was saying, even in what I did not clearly understand. I accepted my inability to understand his thoughts. It was like listening to a language I didn't yet know well. He showed interest in my drawings and I hoped he might be looking for someone to illustrate his work.

After talking to him a couple of times at Mileva's, I was invited to visit him. Mrs. Mileva walked with me and I noticed her distress. She said Radomir was about to enter a hospital, probably for a length of time. He certainly looked haggard. Radomir wanted me to take his files for safekeeping while he was away from his one-room apartment. He was afraid someone might get hold of them, he said. If he were released from the hospital, I was to return his unopened files. I knew what his message meant; I was not to open the package if he lived. Mrs. Mileva seemed very sad, not at all surprised that I was to take care of the papers. Her relationship with him was different.

Radomir's files consisted of a bulk of rarely used folders. They looked almost new, yet he must have had them for a long time, maybe from before the war. One couldn't buy such fine cardboard in the deprived economy of the postwar era. Paper of any kind was a commodity one could hardly ever acquire. When Radomir handed me the carefully tied parcel, it was like being entrusted with a treasure. I felt honored.

He died in the hospital. Soon afterward, Mrs. Mileva left the city. She had completely changed, dramatically aged in a short time. Though she promised to stay in touch with us, we did not hear from her again.

It took me several months to gather the courage to open Radomir's parcel. There were some twenty cream-colored folders, neatly tied with brown ribbon. Each folder contained several pictures. Most were prints cut out from journals. They seemed to have been made before the war. I could figure this out because in our postwar era, there were no publications on the newsstands with such quality prints.

No writing of any kind accompanied the illustrations in Radomir's folders. I was extremely puzzled; there was no way for me to comprehend what the picture files meant.

During the war, my sister and I used to create crossword puzzles, and when we met, we would exchange our inventions in order to keep our minds active. I now tried to deal with Radomir's files like an enigma to be solved. What did the particular illustrations mean? Was there a common key or pattern of meaning that was possible to interpret? As much as I tried, I could not understand what had been so important in his life—all that neat classification of particular cutouts. I couldn't find any rhyme or reason for all the pictures he had collected and held close with such ardor for so long.

From time to time I would go over the folders, driven by mixed sentiments. I liked the thrill of eventually solving the hidden, challenging the unknown. After a while, I began to suspect that Radomir must have been badly damaged in some way by the war.

Had there ever been a manuscript, or had the words never been written? His whole project seemed to have existed only in his mind. No one but he could possibly have understood where the illustrations could fit in the story that existed in his imagination.

Maybe, because in a way he felt kinship with me, he believed that I would understand what the files meant. I too didn't talk much, expressing myself mostly in drawings. Radomir was confident that I would be able to understand the pictures and translate them into whatever his story was supposed to be. The pictures were a collection of isolated images from his past, images that might have evoked memories of events from his life. They were not my memories.

I have read many books over the years. Some I remember vaguely, if at all, as they have left nothing significant for me to think about. Few remained meaningful. Radomir left me the volume of his life for safekeeping. Unlike other books, his unwritten story occupies a space on my memory shelf, and sometimes that untold story emerges when I'm searching for something else from the past.

It was years later, when the cardboard started to disintegrate, that I threw out the folders. Radomir had entrusted me with something so important to him, his memories. He must have considered me a close friend. I believe Radomir must have suffered a terrible personal loss during the war. And then the greatest damage in his life befell him: he lost his words.

the utmost loneliness
is to face a fallen God
how to rid oneself or dispose of
passion no one can define
where is the line that does not exist
yet vibrates like a tight string
between thought and need

DIALOGUE

WHEN MY TIME COMES I'll go with no complaints." I remember him saying that. For me, a young person with a Holocaust history, the termination of life was a rationally accepted fact. We were sitting on low stools in the doorway of the tiny cubicle he called his workshop. It was in one of the old stone buildings at the end of a street, in the ancient part of Safed that faced the deep Galilee valley in the west.

I had come to the street drawn by the brilliance of the sunset, a wish to come closer—to capture more of that fleeting instant when our world is hurtling through a black universe according to an inexorable law.

When I first visited the hills of Galilee, I sensed why, throughout history, that place had drawn people like a magnet, to seek a connection to that inexplicable law, the same law that makes us believe, if not understand as well, the mystery of our existence. On my first visit, years ago, still in my teens, I knew I would be back. Now I was in Safed again. The dry summer heat was filled with the buzz of bees and smell of salvia that grew in abundance on the hills. My mind floated in the haze that enveloped the area like an amniotic sac.

It was on my stroll through the ancient Jewish quarter that I met old Isik. That was a week ago. Now the shop was closed. When I knocked at the door, a woman looking out the window on the second floor simply said: "He is gone to his world." It took me some time to grasp what this meant in Hebrew: "He is gone to his world." She had said this in a voice that could have meant that he was just around the corner. Maybe he was.

It was the hour before the sudden, startling nightfall. We used to sit and watch the light change. Here it seemed so dramatic compared to the long evenings where I grew up, almost a miracle. Colors erupted over the western horizon—and then just as abruptly, the light would be gone.

Never before was I so intrigued by someone much older than I. It was not difficult for me to communicate with Isik, although my Hebrew was inadequate and his Yiddish sounded so different from what I was used to. There wasn't so much to talk about anyway. That part of his face not covered with his almost white unruly beard was deeply lined. He looked solemn. Only his eyes had an amused twinkle that bordered on mockery.

I believe he must have been amused by his own precarious position. It was only the complete acceptance of life's paradoxes that could create such smiling eyes. It must be one of the shortcomings of youth; I could not imagine Isik as a young man, nor myself being his age. From the little he said about himself, Isik must have been my age when he moved away from his family and familiar surroundings in Jerusalem, where his father, he, and his children were born. Isik mentioned all this in the same way he would give information about the olive trees growing in the ravine in front of us.

I wondered what kind of business Isik ran in his shop, especially because there was no indication of any specific activity in the place. There were books and piles of old newspapers in the far corner, almost reaching the low ceiling. Isik seemed surprised when I asked what he was doing.

"I am repairing standing clocks—those with chimes. They are rare nowadays," he added.

I believe his whole business must have slowed down, because there were no signs of any repaired items, tools, or furniture. Anyway, he didn't seem to care for worldly goods very much. His meals must have been frugal as well, judging by his haggard appearance. Now he was gone.

Walking toward Isik's shop just a short while ago, I was thinking of what I wanted to talk to him about. I climbed the steep street. There was a rivulet of water cascading in the narrow space between the sidewalks. The water was caressing the cobblestones, leaving them sparkling smooth. This street must have been built many centuries ago, probably in Roman times. I felt amazed at the affinity I felt, walking here. I was the child of generations born and educated in a different world, yet here I was experiencing an inner dimension that felt as old as the hills around me. I felt an irrational belonging, a kinship with this place and with the man who was giving me answers to questions I did not even have to ask.

Most of my questions dealt with the time before I was born. I could not conceive how people who had witnessed the unimaginable period of our history could find peace and balance. Martin Buber's words would not leave my mind: "The most difficult thing to imagine is reality." Isik was part of that reality, and I was curious how a man like him perceived events that were so incomprehensible. I asked him and there was a long pause in our conversation. Maybe I shouldn't have been that blunt. Emotions and thoughts whirled through my mind. It took a long time before Isik started to talk—slowly.

"I used to have a close relationship with the eternal power that had sheltered me and my forefathers. During the Holocaust I started to dispute with God. I could no longer pray. I turned deaf to the voice that had comforted me throughout my childhood. I was shattered. My love for God was killed, along with the six million Jews who had perished. I received no consolation anymore from my prayers." Isik was sad, not angry.

Yesterday I roamed the hills to get a wider view of the surroundings. Within that day Isik was gone. Now I was looking at the closed door. As a child I used to be fascinated by meteorites that one could barely glimpse and barely get an inkling of having seen. Isik had died and, in accordance with tradition, was buried the same day. During our talks, I had asked him about the reason for immediate burial at a time and in an age when one need not be afraid of pestilence anymore.

He smiled. "The law to bury the dead before sundown comes from the fact that daylight helps us to see reality more clearly; in darkness it is easier to deceive ourselves. The longer we wait to face and realize truth, the stronger the bond becomes with what is dead—not only with a person who is gone, but with the feeling that has already ceased as well. We stay with it and do not notice that it died a long time ago. It is good to bury what is gone."

I remember Isik's face, his head slightly turned to the side, as if listening intensely. He wasn't talking to me; I just happened to be present.

"The image of man made in God's own image. The cruel pitiless human, justifying atrocities—and God, indifferent about his monstrously faulty invention. Or did we invent God to suit our merciless blind nature? I can no longer follow the verbal glorification of prayers. I lost my love, my admiration and fear—all the ingredients needed for absolute obedience. I could not find an explanation for and have lost my acceptance of divine blamelessness. I could not pray, nor can I ever again," he said.

I asked Isik whether he buried God years ago but could not stop mourning. His smile expanded from his eyes until it lit up his whole face: "God is alive; I am the one who is dead. I withdrew from the source of wisdom. I stopped learning. The Talmud says that if you stop learning even for just one day, wisdom moves the distance of two days away from you. When we stop learning, we retreat, while life and wisdom move ahead. The distance grows into opposite directions. It took me a while to realize I was too far away and had lost my direction. Then I died."

Purple light bathed the windows on the upper floor of the stone facade, but it was fading. A gleam of the setting sun was reflected on the cobblestones, polished by centuries of rain and hurrying feet. Isik's door was closed. In the one day I had not visited him, we parted in opposite directions.

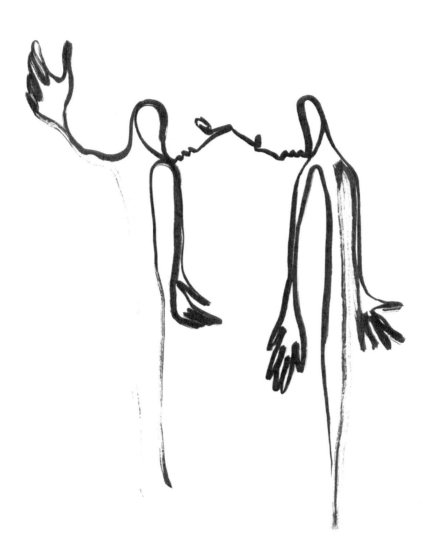

roads leading misleading somewhere anywhere
crossing distressing moving opposite
on different levels
parallel
and as such will never touch
the approaching path distant winding turning
yearning to abandon the trail
that fails to alter life
stale
from trotting the circle
scattered lines fading in twilight
leaving traces that glimmer dimmer
after the shine has gone
in darkness they might be drawn
to each other
in an instant time lock

FAREWELL

I HAD TO GO TO NOVI SAD, to deal with family property, including the house that had been put in my name and my sister's. It was early spring 1949, a transitional moment of the postwar era in Yugoslavia. Life was so different from everything that had seemed familiar just ten years earlier.

I went to my hometown to renounce ownership of all of those pieces of Yugoslavia that remained my inheritance and sign it over to the government. My sister's part belonged to her husband. I had already helped him to claim and receive her share as compensation for what he had done to help us during the war.

The legal proceedings regarding our property took years. I had to recover land deeds and establish death certificates for my grandmother, father, and sister. It took countless hours waiting in municipal offices, often with no one willing to move the procedures along. Because I had to travel about sixty miles north from Belgrade to Novi Sad, I only came up during my vacations from work. Between finishing my studies and making a living, there was no other time to do it all. In addition to the pressure on my time, those trips were also a burdensome tax on my meager earnings. Nonetheless, if I wanted something done, I had to go there, always dreading the journey. This trip was to be the last time I would be in the place where I grew up. I felt as though I were visiting a cemetery where no one whom I cared for was buried.

Renouncing everything of value I owned was the price of my freedom. It was the only way I could legally leave a country that had become more and more alien. But giving up everything that represented security was no novelty for me. The war and four years of experiences since had prepared me well for an atmosphere that was veering on the very edge of hostility toward Jews. My alertness to that fact heightened as my understanding of the world matured.

Back in 1944, shortly after the liberation of Belgrade, I had asked for a special permit from the Partisan Armed Forces to travel with a Soviet medical convoy heading north. My goal was to find my father and grandmother, who I hoped were still alive in occupied Hungary. The war was not yet over.

I remember that journey well. I was sitting in an open truck with several Russian soldiers. We were passing battlefields where only recently there must have been military encounters and fierce fighting. Bodies of slain soldiers, dead horses, and demolished armor mingled in a terrible embrace. Still smoldering fires, the eerie sounds of distant guns, and the stench of war were around us. I didn't know on which side the dead belonged. After battles, death unifies uniforms.

The soldiers beside me did not react at all. I had been forewarned that I should delay my journey, but I wanted to see if Father and Grandmother might be alive in Novi Sad, which at this point had reverted back from Hungary to a liberated Yugoslavia.

After a couple of hours driving through the horror and devastation on and off the completely demolished road, we came to a halt. Everyone went to find a place to relieve himself. I didn't dare move away from the truck; I was afraid to be left behind, alone in the field of corpses.

The officer sitting with the driver in the cab approached me. To my surprise, he introduced himself as the doctor of the unit—and started to talk to me in Yiddish. From my documents he had seen the reason for my journey and that I was Jewish as well. He told me that no one in his unit knew that he was a Jew and then asked me not to say anything about my identity to the soldiers with whom I shared the space.

I was shivering from the cold and the sights, not to mention the stench of the past few hours. The doctor gave me his fur coat to wrap myself in. I felt very grateful. No one had been kind to me in many years.

We parted in Novi Sad with a handshake. And now I was left with puzzled thoughts about the Soviet doctor. He had been reluctant to reveal to his comrades in combat that he was a Jew. Something was very wrong.

Upon arriving in Novi Sad on this trip, I was also soon bewildered by my own existence. Maybe this was because of what had happened in this country since its liberation from Nazi occupation. I introduced myself at the headquarters of the local partisan command and asked if there was any evidence of my father's and grandmother's whereabouts. First, of course, I had gone to the house where we had all lived before the war. There, my worst fears became reality.

As the war moved from the Soviet Union, it burst with new force into neighboring countries like Hungary that had collaborated with the Nazi occupiers. Jews who had escaped the earlier roundups were inevitably caught by the Germans and deported. Father and Grandmother were in those last trains to the camps. And then their property was confiscated by the German military. Our house, located in a nice part of town, consisted of two large apartments. I heard what had happened from the tenant who lived on the second floor. When Grandmother and Father were deported to the camps, the Nazis moved in and made an office out of the confiscated apartment. Then, when the partisans came into the city, they took whatever was left in the apartment and ransacked the place.

The tenant was a frightened Hungarian widow. She was allowed to stay in the maid's quarters and had only moved back into her own apartment when the fighting armies were gone. Upon my arrival in Novi Sad, I went to see her, and she invited me to stay with her. Since there was no other place for me to go, I felt deeply grateful for her gesture. Not one person who had been a friend before the war had made such an offer. Even those people who had known me since childhood seemed afraid somehow to invite me. I made the assumption that I probably didn't fit in to anyone's home. It must have been that I looked in much worse shape than I believed myself to be.

I was viewed with suspicion. When I asked, no one knew what had happened to my folks or was willing to give me information. On the other hand, complete strangers were generous in their attitude toward me. One of them was this neighbor, a woman we hardly knew, who not only gave me shelter but had taken responsibility for putting some of my father's suits and valuables into safekeeping. Before the deportation, Grandmother had also left our Persian carpets and fine china with her.

During the war, a changeover in Hungary's administration produced threats even for non-Jewish residents. The German army, which took over from the Hungarian administration, drove many young Hungarians to join the resistance forces. This was the case with the son of the woman who invited me to stay with her. She feared the partisans, even though her son was part of a unit fighting the Nazi soldiers. The war was not over yet.

The tenant also told me that Grandmother's furniture and everything else from the apartment had been taken to a warehouse by the partisan forces. She suggested that I might identify some of the items, and in that way I might be able to get them back and perhaps sell them. As it turned out, I didn't reclaim any of our family's furniture. All I found was what that nice Hungarian woman had taken care of and now offered me.

I left her most of what she had been entrusted with, taking just the photographs and small mementos I could carry. She also gave me information that I took to the partisan general command. Maybe they had more data about my family in their files. I have never forgotten the officer who looked first at my papers, then at me, and said, "Interesting—the Jews are already returning."

Instantly, with rising hope, I asked: "Who is back?"

The man's face flushed and he slowly responded, "You are the first."

I knew then the liberation was not meant for me.

I did not want to move back to Novi Sad. Father and Grandmother were gone. Our family house was now just brick walls.

In the years that followed, a cumulative process of events made my home country intolerable for me. All my hopes of rebuilding a shattered part of my life became more and more unrealistic. There was no one I could go to for any help. I had to take care of my mother because for her, this had been one war too many. She never got over losing her child and husband.

For me the most important point of my future was to finish the studies that had been interrupted by the war. I graduated from the Academy of Art and, after finding a job, succeeded at my work. Not the least of it was that I managed to make a life for myself and my mother. My industry and dedication were appreciated by those in charge, and as my position developed into one of more responsibility and recognition, I was asked to join the Communist Party. While this was considered an honor, in this evolving political moment the invitation was also a minefield. I was very careful in the way I expressed my appreciation for the nomination, claiming not to be ready for the honor. This strategy bought me some time, but I knew I was being watched from then on. I was not forgiven for turning down the nomination.

Then, slowly, I found myself isolated at my office, given a room alone and no real project to work on. It was obvious that I didn't belong. I knew I never would. There was no one to be with or share opinions with, no one to confide in about how to structure my life or even to exchange views of artistic concepts and expressions. In the postwar Communist domain, the art field was archaic. I kept that opinion to myself.

I had my dreams but kept those a secret as well. I couldn't even trust the person I was in love with; he had no clue about where my mind was. When I visited his home, some of his relatives would call out to him: "Your Jew is here." They didn't mean to be derogatory; they were just very simple people. When I went to say good-bye to his parents just before my mother and I left for Israel, his mother cried and asked me to reconsider the move. His father couldn't understand why I was leaving a good position at work in order to go to a desert country, and one, moreover, that was at war with all its surrounding neighbors.

My lover didn't believe I was going to leave him and the country. He didn't really know me. I was in love, but we were never honestly intimate as human beings. I could never trust him. This was my state of mind during my last trip to Novi Sad. I was there with one single purpose: to sign legal papers. There was no one to say good-bye to.

After a day of traipsing up and down so many staircases in municipal buildings and after signing a multitude of documents, I was drained. At that moment, what I looked forward to was the luxury of staying overnight in a hotel instead of traveling back to Belgrade in the dark. Ordinarily, I would have had my dinner in the room, eating out of a paper bag in my improvised way. But at the end of that day I gave myself the additional luxury of a meal in the hotel restaurant. I wanted to sit at a table, as though that would endow me with some dignity. While in the dining room, indulging myself in an unfamiliar way, I noticed someone standing across from my table; it was a man I knew only as Little Brother. I remembered that the nickname had seemed funny to me when we were first introduced at work in Belgrade a year or two ago. He was very tall and serene and his image didn't fit his being addressed as "Buddy." And yet everybody called him that. He asked if he could join me—it would be nice to have dinner together. I was surprised when he approached me; it was the first time we had ever talked to each other. In fact, we had not even seen each other for a couple of months.

At work, if we met in the corridors we would only occasionally have exchanged hellos. We both worked at a large government enterprise. He was in the weekly news department, mostly writing. My work consisted of building architectural models or details of theatrical sets that would substitute for the larger ones in the film studios. With these different assignments, Buddy and I didn't really have any contact at work or anyplace else.

Before he was transferred to Novi Sad he had heard that I had resigned from my job. We both knew that being transferred to a small town was a kind of exile—a demotion for him. He didn't mind, he said; in fact, he welcomed the isolation. It would give him more opportunity to write. He wanted to know why I had left. I completely lacked the skill of small talk, but after almost eight years of my own silent existence, I had developed a keen ear. Just as musicians can detect a false ringing sound, I could distinguish lies from truth. Little Brother did not try to get information from me. Everything he said and did told me he was sincere. Here was someone who was an isolated island—just like me. The difference was that I had made a decision to abandon isolation—I wanted to move away from being disconnected. And so I was leaving for Israel, where no one was going to call me Jew. As long as I had the chance, I would no longer stay in a place that didn't want me.

Making this break meant that I had given away any and all symbols of security. I'd abandoned a career in my profession. I'd let go of the man I had fallen in love with two years before and was still emotionally involved with; and just a couple of hours ago, I'd signed away all the real estate I owned, relinquishing it to the government I opposed.

Strangely, I felt happy to have thrown all of these things away. They had become burdens; they were hindering my freedom. I couldn't stay in a place that was trying to change the core of my being. Years of starvation, hard work, and fear had left me with a determination not to yield to any force that was out to break my mind.

Despite the enormously destructive effort of the Nazi doctrine to strip me of my dignity and free thinking, they were left almost unimpaired. I wasn't going to let the Communists destroy my will either.

Maybe it was my ignorance that led me not to consider life's oppressive forces. I had discarded everything I had. It never entered my mind that I had thrown away everything in exchange for taking a serious risk. I was going to an unknown place and building a new life, with no one to ask for advice about what and how to do it. When the war started, I had made a bold move, but now my life was not really endangered. In peril was my choice of how to live.

There was a long silence when I told Buddy about my leaving for Israel. His reaction surprised me. He reached across the table and took both my hands in his. The way he looked at me that first moment startled me—making me think he was going to kiss my hands in the middle of the restaurant. In postwar Yugoslavia something like that would have been unthinkable. As if reading my mind, he smiled, and then became sad. He held my hands a long time and said: "We're both outcasts, only you have a place to go to. I do not."

As the evening advanced he talked with more ease. He origi-
nally came from rural Serbia, and had been with the partisans
throughout the entire war. I tried to imagine the soft-spoken Buddy
as a fighter all during those very difficult years. It was one of the
faces he kept hidden. Of all those who had joined at the beginning
of that extensive struggle, there were so few survivors. If not the
enemy, then the epidemics took countless lives.

Buddy's whole attitude was so different from that of the few
other war veterans I knew. I was bewildered by his statement that
he was an outcast like me. Why wouldn't he be accepted? After all,
he had fought for the political power now ruling the country.

It was getting late and the dining room was almost empty when
Buddy quietly told me why he didn't fit into Yugoslav society and
had no place to go. He was homosexual. This time it was I who
reached across the table and held his hands. It had taken a great deal
of trust for him to reveal that. Even the slightest suspicion was dangerous. Homosexuality was not talked about, and if rumors started,
people were jailed or just disappeared. Before the war the attitude
was unforgiving; after the war homosexuality became totally unac-
ceptable. I felt honored by his trust, and it occurred to me that I was
being more intimate with this man I was talking to for the first time
in my life than I ever was with my lover of two years.

The dining room emptied, and it was time for us to get up and
leave. Buddy walked me to my room and I was not surprised when
he asked me if he could just stay with me for the rest of the night. I
knew that if he spent the night in my room it could help him silence
any possible rumors. That he had dined with and stayed overnight
with a woman would have been noticed and probably registered.
Our connection could silence suspicion and give him some time.

I didn't mind. We shared loneliness and his life-threatening secret. It was part of a relationship that existed only for a couple of
hours but with trust for a lifetime.

It must have been early morning when he left the room. I didn't
wake up. It was still dark when the alarm rang and I had to hurry to
catch my bus. I had paid for my room the day before, but there was
no time for coffee. I was glad that Buddy had left; there was nothing

more for us to say to each other. It was only respect for the trust and understanding of isolation and alienation, of not belonging, that had created the closeness between us.

He was going to be my one cherished memory of Novi Sad: falling asleep and being hugged by someone who was as isolated from society as I was, a human being with an overwhelming need to share an extremely dangerous secret. It felt good to have had the opportunity to reciprocate his trust.

The bus station was close by and I took a seat. Then, as I lowered the window, I saw Buddy hurrying toward the bus. He handed me some rolled-up newspapers. Unshaven, he looked drawn and old. I was moved that he had brought the papers—it was so thoughtful of him to provide me with reading material for the ride. When I saw the flowers—still bright with morning dew in the damp paper—I was overwhelmed. The way they looked and were wrapped, I knew that Buddy must have taken them from somebody's garden.

We were both smiling—as we must have both forgotten how to cry—when he kissed my hand.

About the Author

Ava Kadishson Schieber was born in Novi Sad, a city near Belgrade. Her mother was a convert to Judaism. Her father changed his name in order to receive a commission in the Austro-Hungarian army during the First World War. Schieber grew up in Novi Sad and then moved in 1940 to Belgrade, where the family prospered until the Nazis invaded Belgrade in 1941. Schieber went into hiding with relatives of her sister's fiancé, who was Serbian. She lived with them on an isolated farm for four years, after which she was reunited with her mother. Her father and sister did not survive the war. Schieber moved with her mother to Israel after the war but has been living in Chicago for the past twenty years.